Divine Invitation of Jesus

Published by Redemptorist Publications
Wolf's Lane, Chawton, Hampshire, GU34 3HQ, UK

Tel. +44 (0)1420 88222
Email: customercare@rpbooks.co.uk
www.rpbooks.co.uk

A registered charity limited by guarantee.
Registered in England 03261721

First published October 2024

Edited by Helen Birkbeck
Designed by Eliana Thompson

ISBN 978-0-85231-644-3

All rights reserved. No part of this publication may be reproduced, stored in a retrieval system, or transmitted in any form or by any means, electronic, mechanical, photocopying, recording or otherwise, without prior permission in writing from Redemptorist Publications.

Copyright © Jim McManus, 2024

The moral right of Jim McManus to be identified as the author of this work has been asserted in accordance with the Copyright, Designs and Patents Act 1988.

A CIP catalogue record for this book is available from the British Library.

Every effort has been made to trace copyright holders and to obtain their permission for the use of copyright material. The publisher apologises for any errors or omissions and would be grateful for notification of any corrections that should be incorporated in future reprints or editions of this book.

The publisher gratefully acknowledges permission to use the following copyright material:

Excerpts from the New Revised Standard Version of the Bible: Anglicised Edition, © 1989, 1995, Division of Christian Education of the National Council of the Churches of Christ in the United States of America. Used by permission. All rights reserved.

Other Scripture versions used:

The New Jerusalem Bible, published and copyright 1985 by Darton, Longman & Todd Ltd and Les Editions du Cerf, and used by permission of the publishers.

Printed and bound by Bishops Printers Ltd, Walton Rd, Drayton, Portsmouth PO6 1TR

The Divine Invitation of Jesus

Experiencing
the Lord's presence
in your life

OTHER TITLES BY JIM MCMANUS C.SS.R.

Hallowed Be Thy Name: a spirituality for today
(London: Darton, Longman & Todd Ltd, 1996)

All Generations Will Call Me Blessed
(Independent Publishers Group, 1999)

Healing in the Spirit
(Chawton, Hampshire: Redemptorist Publications, 2002)

The Inside Job: a spirituality of true self-esteem
(Chawton, Hampshire: Redemptorist Publications, 2004)

The Healing Power of the Sacraments
(Chawton, Hampshire: Redemptorist Publications, 2005)

Finding Forgiveness: personal and spiritual perspectives
(with Dr Stephanie Thornton) (Chawton, Hampshire: Redemptorist Publications, 2005)

Searching for Serenity: spirituality in later life (with Dr Stephanie Thornton)
(Chawton, Hampshire: Redemptorist Publications, 2010)

I Am My Body: Blessed Pope John Paul's theology of the body
(Chawton, Hampshire: Redemptorist Publications, 2011)

Going to Mass: becoming the Eucharist we celebrate
(Chawton, Hampshire: Redemptorist Publications, 2015)

Fountain of Grace: celebrating 150 years of the icon of love
(Chawton, Hampshire: Redemptorist Publications, 2015)

Embraced by Mercy: God's ultimate gift
(Chawton, Hampshire: Redemptorist Publications, 2015)

At Home in the Mysteries of Christ: the grace of the Rosary
(Chawton, Hampshire: Redemptorist Publications, 2016)

Our Spiritual Lifeline: the oxygen of Christian prayer
(Chawton, Hampshire: Redemptorist Publications, 2017)

Sent to Proclaim the Gospel: honouring the legacy of St Paul VI
(Chawton, Hampshire: Redemptorist Publications, 2018)

Talking about Jesus: our call to everyday evangelisation (With Bill Horton)
(Chawton, Hampshire: Redemptorist Publications, 2020)

Keeping Faith Fully Alive: igniting the flame of faith (Ebook only)
(Chawton, Hampshire: Redemptorist Publications, 2022)

	Preface	6
Chapter 1	Make your home in me	9
Chapter 2	God the Father makes his home with us	23
Chapter 3	Jesus, remember me	39
Chapter 4	The gift of the Holy Spirit	51
Chapter 5	Baptism: Born again of water and the Holy Spirit	66
Chapter 6	Making our home in Christ through the Eucharist	81
Chapter 7	The sacrament of reconciliation and healing	98
Chapter 8	Jesus' last words to us from the cross – "She is your mother"	112

PREFACE

Jesus showed us how to make our home in him when he said, "Those who love me will keep my word, and my Father will love them, and we will come to them and make our home with them" (John 14:23). God the Father and his Son, Jesus Christ, make their home in us and in gratitude for this divine presence in our hearts we can now make our home in Jesus. Jesus is our Lord and Saviour, but he is also our brother. And he says to us, "Abide in me as I abide in you. Just as the branch cannot bear fruit by itself unless it abides in the vine, neither can you unless you abide in me. I am the vine, you are the branches. Those who abide in me and I in them bear much fruit, because apart from me you can do nothing" (John 15:4-5).

Jesus alerts us to our total dependence on him when he says "apart from me you can do nothing". To reiterate: Jesus is our Lord and Saviour, but he is also our God and our brother. He loves us so much that he willingly died a cruel death on the cross for us.

Deep down in our hearts we believe that without the abiding presence of the Holy Spirit, we would never be able to respond to Jesus' invitation to "make our home in him" or "abide in him".

Throughout the Gospels Jesus encourages us to make our home in him. But it is not a one-way movement. He makes a home in each one of us who loves him. We listen again to his words: "Those who love me will keep my word, and my Father will love them, and we will come to them and make our home with them" (John 14:23). What an extraordinary revelation! What an awe-inspiring love God has for each one of us! God our Father and his Son, Jesus Christ, make their home in our hearts; they want to be present in our lives; we are God's children and Jesus is our Saviour and Brother. As we welcome the divine presence of God the Father and Jesus Christ into our hearts, we will be given the grace to make our home in Jesus. We will be able to abide in the Lord.

I have met many good Christians who love their faith and are faithful in following Jesus, but who have missed out on Jesus' invitation to make their home in him. They unconsciously keep

Christ at a distance. Christ is "up in heaven". They believe with their whole heart that God is in heaven but they haven't as yet realised that God's heaven is also in the human heart. As St Alphonsus Liguori, a great Doctor of the Church and the founder of my religious congregation, the Redemptorists, said, "the paradise of God is the human heart".[1] God our Creator dwells in our hearts. It is Jesus who reveals to us that God the Father makes his home in our hearts. The aim of this book is to help you to ponder the desire in the heart of Jesus to make a home in you, and his invitation to you to make your home in him.

We have eight chapters in this book. Each chapter is an exploration of what it means to make our home in Jesus. I hope that each one will give you the opportunity to reflect on your own relationship with Jesus and how you are making your home in him or remaining in him.

I have been thinking about writing this book on the Lord's words "make your home in me, abide in me" for a long time. As I marked sixty years of being a Redemptorist priest on 12 January 2024, I realised that my time for writing was getting short and so, during the past year, I have been working on this book. Spiritually it has been very helpful to me as I pondered the gift God gives us. My prayer will be that, as you read and reflect on this book, you will gratefully experience the Lord's presence in your life and work and make your home in him.

I am grateful to Michael Brennan, from Australia, who has been a member of St Mary's Monastery for several months. He has been a great help in checking each footnote on each page of the manuscript and in solving problems on my computer. I also wish to thank the Redemptorist members of my community of St Mary's for the spiritual support each of them gives as we meet three times a day for our community prayers.

Jim McManus C.Ss.R.
St Mary's
Kinnoull, Perth PH2 7BP

---

[1] Denis Billy, *Finding Our Way to God* (Liguori, MO: Liguori Publications), 36.

CHAPTER ONE

MAKE YOUR HOME IN ME – CHRIST'S INVITATION

Home is where you know who you are. You are a son or a daughter of the house. You feel at home. You know you belong. That feeling of belonging flows from love. It is love that makes a house a home. Without love, a house, no matter how elegant, can never be a home. Love alone creates the atmosphere that upgrades the house into a home. It is love that creates the spiritual foundation on which the home can be built. I still vividly remember the distress in a man as he shared with me the loss of his wife and family. He said, "I worked day and night to make the money to run my own business and build my own house so that my family would have a beautiful place to live in, but I was too preoccupied with my own ambitions to pay attention to them and share my love with them, and now I have lost them." They had left him. He was broken-hearted. The beautiful house and stacks of money were no substitute for his love. Without that love, the family didn't feel at home with him.

Jesus says to each of us, "Those who love me will keep my word, and my Father will love them, and we will come to them and make our home with them" (John 14:23). God wants to make his home in our hearts. This is an amazing and life-giving revelation. Jesus invites us to make our home in him. He says, "Abide in me as I abide in you. Just as the branch cannot bear fruit by itself unless it abides in the vine, neither can you unless you abide in me. I am the vine, you are the branches. Those who abide in me and I in them bear much fruit, because apart from me you can do nothing" (John 15:4-5). These words of the Lord invite us and indeed warn us not to rely on our own good intentions or purposes. That is why he says to us *apart from me* you can do nothing". I may have many good intentions, but if I am not seeking the Lord's support, "abiding in him", or, as other translations say, "remaining in him", my good intentions will not materialise. That man who lost his family became fully aware of his big mistake in life – without Christ, he could do nothing in the realm of true love. But Jesus came to save him and heal his broken heart. The Lord's life-giving words are spoken for our growth in the spiritual life.

What an awe-inspiring love God has for each one of us! God our Father and his Son, Jesus Christ, want to make their home in our hearts; they want to be present in our lives. Our earthly parents may have brought us into this world but the person each of us is was created by God. God's very first words in the Bible are "Let us make humankind in our image, according to our likeness" (Genesis 1:26). We can easily overlook this amazing revelation of how God sees us, loves us and is with us throughout our life on this earth. We are made in God's image and likeness.

Believers can unconsciously keep God at a distance while they keep praying to God "up in heaven". As St Alphonsus Liguori said, "the paradise of God is the human heart". That is where our God dwells, in our hearts. When we turn to God in prayer, we shouldn't try to get out of ourselves into the pure light of God. Rather, we enter the depths of our being, our very heart, to be with God our Father and his Son, Jesus Christ, who make their home in our heart. Jesus, the Son of God who assumed our human nature and was born of the Virgin Mary by the power of the Holy Spirit, invites us to make our home in him. Christ's invitation to us to make our home in him requires that we meditate on both the humanity and the divinity of Jesus. The Son of God became a human being and was born of the Virgin Mary by the power of the Holy Spirit so that we sinful human beings could share in his divine nature as he now shares in our human nature. At every Mass we pray, "By the mystery of this water and wine may we share in the divinity of Christ who humbled himself to share in our humanity." Our Catholic faith is rich in magnificent doctrines and teachings – excellent liturgy, life-changing spirituality, superb theology and brilliant social ethics, to mention just a few. And yet we can easily overlook the very core of our faith in those amazing words Jesus speaks to us when he says "abide in me", "make your home in me". That is the fundamental invitation Jesus holds out to each of us. Jesus Christ is our Redeemer. The fruit of our redemption, which he won for us on the cross at Calvary, is that we can now be at home in him. He gave his life for us so that we can share our life with him. That is why he says to us, "Blessed … are those who hear the word of God and obey it" (Luke 11:28).

Our life's primary task is to gratefully accept Christ's invitation and make our home in him. He will teach us how to find and achieve the meaning and the purpose of our life. Through the Holy Spirit who lives in our hearts we will learn the deeper meaning of making our home in Christ. As St Paul says, "He is the image of the invisible God, the firstborn of all creation… He is the head of the body, the church; he is the beginning, the firstborn from the dead… For in him all the fullness of God was pleased to dwell" (Colossians 1:15, 18, 19). Reflect on what St Paul says: since the fullness of God dwells in Christ, when we make our home in Christ we are dwelling in the fullness of God. This is where we find our inner peace, the forgiveness of our sins, the grace to love everyone in our life (even our enemies), the willingness and readiness to share our faith with others.

At the Last Supper, in his great prayer to the Father, Jesus said, "This is eternal life, that they may know you, the only true God, and Jesus Christ whom you have sent" (John 17:3). The surest way to get to know Jesus Christ is to accept his invitation and make our home in him. Each of us will have our own personal experience of making our home in Christ. No matter where we are and no matter what we are doing, we must personally remind ourselves that we are doing it in Christ. We must also be on our guard not to allow our failures to undermine our faith in Christ's presence and his willingness to welcome us back into his presence. Christ knows our weaknesses. When we fall, he is there to pick us up again. Christ is the fulfilment of all the promises God made to us, his sinful people. He is the fulfilment of this consoling promise:

> I will sprinkle clean water upon you, and you shall be clean from all your uncleannesses, and from all your idols I will cleanse you. A new heart I will give you, and a new spirit I will put within you; and I will remove from your body the heart of stone and give you a heart of flesh. I will put my spirit within you, and make you follow my statutes and be careful to observe my ordinances.
>
> Ezekiel 36:25-27

Each of us has to apply this great promise to ourselves. Take some time to ask yourself: do I need Christ to pour the cleansing water of the Holy Spirit to purify and sanitise my inner being? Do I need the new heart that Christ is offering me? Do I want Christ to give me his Spirit? Do I need Christ to remove from my body the heart of stone and give me a new heart?

The first thing we have to do when we ask Christ a question is to listen for his response. He will always respond, but in God's way. God says, "Be still, and know that I am God!" (Psalm 46:10). It is in stillness and quietness that our heart is prepared to hear God's word. It is in our heart, not in our mind, that we will hear what God has to say. As the psalm says, "Let me hear what God the Lord will speak, for he will speak peace to his people, to his faithful, to those who turn to him in their hearts" (Psalm 85:8). Turning to God in our hearts means withdrawing our hearts from loving what is offensive to God. We cannot come into God's presence if our heart is still turned away from God. Once we turn to

God and enter his presence, we experience joy. We can say with the psalmist, "In your presence there is fullness of joy" (Psalm 16:11). With this "fullness of joy" in God's presence, we will have the confidence and trust to "abide in him" and wait patiently for the word that God will speak in our heart.

The heart is the seat of love

Jesus tells us that it is with our heart that we must love God. A Pharisee lawyer asked him, "Teacher, which commandment in the law is the greatest?" Jesus said to him: "You shall love the Lord your God with all your heart, and with all your soul, and with all your mind. This is the greatest and first commandment. And a second is like it: 'You shall love your neighbour as yourself'" (Matthew 22:36-40). And, in case we are tempted to settle for loving only those who love us, Jesus says, "I say this to you who are listening: Love your enemies; do good to those who hate you; bless those who curse you; pray for those who treat you badly" (Luke 6:27-28, NJB). Love is at the heart of the Gospel of our salvation. It is that love which the Lord Jesus wants to give to us as we make our home in him. We cannot be at home with Jesus while we refuse to forgive an enemy from our heart. We will either turn to the Lord and ask for liberation from our unforgivingness or find another home for cultivating our refusal to forgive.

As I write this chapter in June 2023, reflecting on how Christ invites us to make our home in him, I get sad when I think of the many thousands of refugees – men, women and children – who have lost their lives as they made very dangerous sea journeys to reach a safe place to call their home. Most of them were fleeing from danger in their homeland and were not welcome in other lands. The words of Jesus rang in my ears: "I was hungry and you gave me no food, I was thirsty and you gave me nothing to drink, I was a stranger and you did not welcome me" (Matthew 25:42-43). Pope Francis became the voice of all those refugees as he called on the rich countries of the West to make them welcome and help them to begin a new life in safety. He met with refugees on his pastoral visit to Cyprus and on the Greek island of Lesbos. He was able to arrange for a number of the refugees to come back with him to the Vatican.

Pope Francis with a family of refugees from Afghanistan whom he brought to the Vatican

Jesus himself became a refugee in Egypt shortly after his birth. The three Wise Men from the East came to Jerusalem and asked, "Where is the child who has been born king of the Jews?" (Matthew 2:2). King Herod sent for them and asked them, once they had found the child, to come back and tell him, because he too wanted to go and "and pay him homage". When they had visited the child Jesus in Bethlehem, St Matthew tells us that they were "warned in a dream not to return to Herod [and] they left for their own country by another road" (Matthew 2:12). After they had left, "an angel of the Lord appeared to Joseph in a dream and said, 'Get up, take the child and his mother, and flee to Egypt, and remain there until I tell you; for Herod is about to search for the child, to destroy him.' Then Joseph got up, took the child and his mother by night, and went to Egypt" (Matthew 2:13-14). As we Christians joyfully celebrate the birth of Jesus in a stable in Bethlehem, we should also remember how the Holy Family became refugees and had to seek safety in Egypt. What would have happened if Egypt had closed its borders to refugees? At his audience on 29 December 2021 Pope Francis appealed to all people and said, "Let's think of the many people who are victims of wars, who want to flee from their homeland but cannot; let's think of the migrants who set out on the road to freedom but end up on the street or in the sea; let's think of Jesus in the arms of Joseph and Mary, fleeing, and let us see in him each one of the migrants of today." Jesus put it this way: "Just as you did it to one of the least of these who are members of my family, you did it to me" (Matthew 25:40). For us as Christians, every refugee, every person in need, is our brother or sister. We thank God that in Pope Francis the Christian voice is not silent when people are suffering gross injustice and trying to flee from it. Clearly, he has made his home in Christ and it is in and through Christ that he has the courage to proclaim the rights of the refugees and the duties of countries to help them.

Our home in Christ

Those who make their home in Christ will be directed by the Holy Spirit and will have the courage to stand up for the truth. Speaking about the truth, Jesus says, "If you continue in my word, you are truly my disciples; and you will know the truth, and the truth will make you free" (John 8:31-32). In that one sentence Jesus shows us the path to true freedom. We must be faithful to the word that Christ speaks to us; we must be willing to let go of untruths that may have entered our hearts and we must be eager to learn the truth that Christ wants to teach us. That is why he came into this world. As he said to Pilate, "For this I came into the world, to testify to the truth. Everyone who belongs to the truth listens to my voice" (John 18:37). The truth that Jesus wants to teach us is that he is our Lord and Saviour; that God, his Father, has accepted the offering of himself that he made on the cross for the forgiveness of all our sins; that we are now reconciled with God and accepted as his sons and daughters; that Jesus is now our brother; and that with Jesus we are now the family of God. The Holy Spirit will teach us, day by day, how to live and apply this truth to ourselves. Then we will begin to see ourselves as God sees us. We will begin to let go of all negativity about ourselves and others. We will experience the peace that Jesus wants us to have when he says, "Peace I leave with you; my peace I give to you. I do not give to you as the world gives. Do not let your hearts be troubled, and do not let them be afraid" (John 14:27).

When we make our home in Christ, he encourages us not to let troubles enter our hearts. Things will go wrong, disappointments will come our way, sicknesses may assail us, but the words of Jesus, "Do not let your hearts be troubled", will echo in our hearts and we will refuse entrance to all troubles. We do that in Jesus' name. However, if you discover that trouble *has* found its way into your heart, don't be disappointed and start condemning yourself. Just turn to the Lord for his help. We have a perfect prayer in the book of Psalms: "Into your hand I commit my spirit; you have redeemed me, O Lord, faithful God" (Psalm 31:5). You can face any problem with that little prayer in your heart. In times of trouble, always remember that you are at home in Christ. That is why you place all troubles, disappointments and illnesses in Christ's hands as you remember his promise: "Peace I leave with you; my peace I give to you" (John 14:27). Thank him for that peace and keep your heart focused on the Lord.

Making our home in Christ provides us with the perfect opening to obtain relief from all the negative and sinful attitudes that may have entered our heart over the years; grudges and resentments, rash judgements and even hatred can contaminate a heart that has suffered much at the hands of others. Being at home in Christ gives us the perfect opportunity for presenting all these to the Lord and asking for his cleansing of our heart. God has promised, "A new heart I will give you, and a new spirit I will put within you" (Ezekiel 36:26). When we make our home in Christ, the wounds of sin in our hearts, inflicted by our own misdeeds or those of others against us, are healed. Christ is the divine physician and he accurately diagnoses what the broken heart needs and how best to heal that wounded heart.

Sadly, many good people often feel that Christ is "up in heaven" and far away. The very fact that he invites us to make our home in him should assure us that, instead of being far away, Christ is just waiting for us to make our home in him. Jesus says, "Listen! I am standing at the door, knocking; if you hear my voice and open the door, I will come in to you and eat with you, and you with me" (Revelation 3:20). We should frequently ask ourselves, "Do I 'open the door' and invite Christ to come in?" God gives us the gift of prayer to enable us to open our heart to receive the gift God wants to give us when our heart feels sad or even broken. It is especially at times like these that we should accept Jesus' invitation and make our home in him. If we nourish unforgivingness, if we secretly seek revenge on someone who has betrayed us, we are inflicting a deeper wound in our heart than the person who hurt us. Christ knows our fragility and that is why he invites us to make our home in him. No one who accepts Christ's invitation will ever feel overcome by the wounds and hurts others can inflict. They begin to see others through the eyes of Jesus, who cried out on his cross, "Father, forgive them; for they do not know what they are doing" (Luke 23:34). In a later chapter we will reflect on the healing power of forgiveness.

Accepting Christ's invitation

The closer people come to Christ, the more they become aware of their sinfulness. A good example is St Peter. Peter and his companions had been fishing all night but had caught nothing. When they came ashore, Jesus was standing by the edge of the water, teaching a large crowd. He got into Peter's boat and asked him to put out a little way from the shore. Then he continued his teaching from Peter's boat. When he had finished speaking, he said to Peter, "Put out into the deep water and let down your nets for a catch" (Luke 5:4). Amazed by this request, Peter replied, "Master, we have worked all night long but have caught nothing. Yet if you say so, I will let down the nets" (Luke 5:5). Peter was the fisherman but he was willing to do what Jesus was asking. St Luke says, "When they had done this, they caught so many fish that their nets were beginning to break" (Luke 5:6). Peter, a seasoned fisherman, "fell down at Jesus' knees, saying, 'Go away from me, Lord, for I am a sinful man!'" (Luke 5:8). What did Jesus say in reply? He said, "Do not be afraid; from now on you will be catching people" (Luke 5:10).

A living hope

When Jesus says to us, "Make your home in me as I make mine in you," we can have the same kind of reaction that Peter had. In the presence of the holiness of Jesus, Peter became aware of his sinfulness. When we become aware of our own sinfulness, we do not withdraw from the presence of Jesus. Rather, it is the very presence of Christ in us that is making us aware that we are sinful people whom Christ has redeemed and whom he is inviting to make our home in him. The Pharisees at the time of Jesus were always criticising him for eating and drinking with those whom they called "sinners". Jesus responded to them with these memorable words: "Those who are well have no need of a physician, but those who are sick; I have come to call not the righteous but sinners" (Mark 2:17). The person who knows that he or she is a sinner and in need of God's mercy is the one who will hear Christ's invitation to "make your home in me as I make mine in you". Christ never gives up on us. If you are struggling with some sinful attitude or habit, always remind yourself that Christ is inviting you to make your home in him and let him deal with your struggles. Draw close to Christ in your prayer and speak to him about your challenges. On your own, you will not be able to deal with them; but with Christ you will be set free and filled with grace and peace. Jesus makes this great promise to us: "Peace I leave with you; my peace I give to you. I do not give to you as the world gives. Do not let your hearts be troubled, and do not let them be afraid" (John 14:27). Once we accept Christ's invitation to make our home in him, we receive the grace to place everything that is going on in our life in his hands; he will teach us how to open our heart to receive his forgiveness, his mercy and his joy. He will give us a living hope. As St Peter says, "Blessed be the God and Father of our Lord Jesus Christ! By his great mercy he has given us a new birth into a living hope through the resurrection of

Jesus Christ from the dead" (1 Peter 1:3). It is this living hope that we need today. We face the future not as defeated human beings, but as God's children, to whom he gives this living hope. Each new day, as we open our heart to God, his gift of living hope within us fills us with peace and confidence and prepares us to become Christ's witnesses in the world.

Getting to know Christ

It is possible to have a great respect for Jesus Christ in heaven, to pray to him every day, but unconsciously to keep him at that distance, in heaven. We know that we are sinful, always in need of God's forgiveness; we may feel at times that only the great saints can get to know Jesus personally and become close to him. Yet Jesus says the opposite. He says, "I have come to call not the righteous but sinners to repentance" (Luke 5:32). And St Paul could say, "Christ Jesus came into the world to save sinners – of whom I am the foremost" (1 Timothy 1:15). Jesus doesn't wait for us to become close to him before he invites us to make our home in him. It is by making our home in Christ that we receive the grace we need to be his disciples, to put all our trust in him and, when we fall again into sin, to turn to him immediately and ask for his forgiveness. The more we get to know Christ personally, the more we will be able to listen to his voice and ask his forgiveness for any sin that we may commit. That is how the Christian peacefully and joyfully lives the life of faith. Pope Benedict XVI put it well:

> Being Christian is not the result of an ethical choice or a lofty idea, but the encounter with an event, a person, which gives life a new horizon and a decisive direction.[1]

That encounter with Christ, that turning to Christ and asking for his mercy and forgiveness, is the first step in getting to know him personally. We do not see him with our

---

1 Pope Benedict XVI, *Deus Caritas Est* ("*God is Love*"), (2006), 1.

eyes but with our heart. And the heart will speak a word of love. It will say, "Jesus, I love you and I thank you for inviting me to make my home in you. I am sorry for all my sins, for having so often ignored your presence in my life." We speak to Christ personally. We put our trust in him and open our hearts to him. We have to keep reminding ourselves that Jesus says to us, "Abide in me as I abide in you. Just as the branch cannot bear fruit by itself unless it abides in the vine, neither can you unless you abide in me. I am the vine, you are the branches" (John 15:4-5). Ponder that intimate relationship that Jesus has with you. You are a branch on the vine that is Christ. The life of the branch comes from the vine. A branch has no life and existence on its own. Yet, on the superficial level, it is the branch, with all its fresh grapes, that people look at. Jesus uses this image of the relationship between the vine and its branches to bring home to us our total dependence on him. We receive all our Christian life through him. Jesus is our life-support system.

As a child of God, each of us has free access to God our Father. We don't have to make an appointment to see him. But it is through Jesus that we come into the Father's presence. Jesus says, "I am the way, and the truth, and the life. No one comes to the Father except through me" (John 14:6). We remind ourselves that Jesus Christ is truly God and truly man. In the mystery of the Holy Trinity, he was sent by God the Father into the world to redeem us human beings from our sins and their consequence, death. He was conceived in his mother's womb and born as the son of Mary by the power of the Holy Spirit. The triune God, Father, Son and Holy Spirit, are actively engaged in the work of our redemption. That is why we begin all our prayers by making the sign of the cross as we say, "In the name of the Father and of the Son and of the Holy Spirit." That is also why we conclude many of our prayers by saying, "Glory be to the Father and to the Son and to the Holy Spirit."

Personal spiritual exercise for internalising the message of this chapter

- Centre yourself; sitting upright; breathing rhythmically; clearing your mind of all preoccupations.
- Bring yourself to bodily stillness.
- Now calmly acknowledge that you are here because God the Father created you in your mother's womb.
- Experience the Father rushing to embrace you and welcome you.
- Be still for some time in the presence of the God of mercy and compassion, and receive his love.
- Now focus again on your breathing as you relax in God's presence.
- And bring yourself gently back to the world.

This spiritual exercise will deepen your awareness of being in the presence of the God of grace and show you how God has embraced you with his love and mercy.

CHAPTER TWO

GOD THE FATHER MAKES HIS HOME WITH US

Speaking about those who love him, Jesus said, "Those who love me will keep my word, and my Father will love them, and we will come to them and make our home with them" (John 14:23). That is a life-changing revelation. Jesus is revealing to us that God the Father, the Creator of the whole universe, will come to those who love Christ our Lord and make his home with them. Our heavenly Father, infinite in holiness, infinite in love, seeks out the human heart that loves Jesus. As St Alphonsus said, "The paradise of God is the human heart."[1] By unfolding this mystery of love to us, Jesus, the incarnate Son of God and the human son of Mary, is inviting us to make our home in them just as they make their home in us. The all-holy God dwells in our sinful hearts so that we can dwell in Christ's sacred heart. This is the mystery of our faith, the mystery of our salvation.

Jesus is the holiness of God and we, his brothers and sisters, are sinful, weak human beings. Yet, out of their infinite love for us, God our Father and Jesus, his beloved Son, want to make a home in our hearts. Trying to analyse this mystery of faith intellectually will produce no results. We have to believe this revelation and ponder it in our hearts. St Paul writes, "If you confess with your lips that Jesus is Lord and believe in your heart that God raised him from the dead, you will be saved. For one believes with the heart and so is justified, and one confesses with the mouth and so is saved" (Romans 10:9-10). We don't believe with our intelligence but with our heart. The heart in question is not the physical organ that pumps the blood through our body but the spiritual core of our being. Your physical body is not the fullness of yourself. You also have a spiritual body, and it is through that spiritual body that we

---

[1] St Alphonsus Liguori, *Ascetical Works of St. Alphonsus* (1696–1787) (New York: Benziger, 1887).

are made in the image and likeness of God. St John said, "God is spirit" (John 4:24), and it is through the human spirit that the person is created in the image and likeness of God.

Jesus says to us, "I am the way, and the truth, and the life. No one comes to the Father except through me" (John 14:6). It is through Jesus that each of us has access to the Father. It takes time for this amazing revelation to permeate our hearts. The infinite, all-holy God who created us, and Jesus Christ the divine Son of God who redeemed us, want to make their home with us. Our immediate response to that revelation is one of wonder and amazement. The very thought of the holiness of God entering our heart makes us aware of our own sinfulness. We might be inclined to say, with the apostle Peter, "Go away from me, Lord, for I am a sinful man!" (Luke 5:8). If we have such anxiety, Jesus responds to us as he did to the Pharisees: "I have come to call not the righteous but sinners" (Mark 2:17). Our greatest saints thought that they were the greatest sinners. As we have seen, St Paul wrote to his co-worker Timothy, "Christ Jesus came into the world to save sinners – of whom I am the foremost" (1 Timothy 1:15). Our sinful nature is no barrier to the all-holy God who wants to make his home with us.

Call to conversion

Jesus calls everyone to conversion. The very first words he spoke in Mark's Gospel are: "The time is fulfilled, and the kingdom of God has come near; repent, and believe in the good news" (Mark 1:15). The good news that Jesus proclaims is that the Father loves us and that he and the Father want to make their home in us because we love him. God could give us no better news than that. Despite our sinfulness and our weakness, Jesus assures us that his love for us washes away all our sins when we ask for his forgiveness. As God said through the prophet Ezekiel:

> I will sprinkle clean water upon you, and you shall be clean
> from all your uncleannesses, and from all your idols I will
> cleanse you. A new heart I will give you, and a new spirit
> I will put within you, and I will remove from your body the
> heart of stone and give you a heart of flesh. I will put my
> spirit within you and make you follow my statutes and be
> careful to observe my ordinances.
>
> Ezekiel 36:25-27

Through Jesus' death and resurrection, every promise God made to his people of the Old Covenant, such as this great promise through the prophet Ezekiel, has been fulfilled. Now God who created us wants to make his home with us.

We dare to call him Father

At the celebration of Mass, the priest introduces the Lord's Prayer with these words: "At the Saviour's command and formed by divine teaching, we dare to say: Our Father, who art in heaven." It was Jesus himself who taught us to call God "our Father". "One of his disciples said to him, 'Lord, teach us to pray, as John taught his disciples.' He said to them, 'When you pray, say: Father, hallowed be your name. Your kingdom come...'" (Luke 11:1-2). We dare to call God our Father because Jesus tells us that we can and *should* speak to God, his Father and ours, in this familial way. It is Jesus who reveals to us that God is our loving Father. He said to his disciples, "No one knows the Son except the Father, and no one knows the Father except the Son and anyone to whom the Son chooses to reveal him" (Matthew 11:27). Jesus has chosen to reveal God the Father to us and he teaches us to call God *our Father*. The fact that we dare to call God our Father is entirely owing to the revelation that we have received in our hearts. It is the gift of faith, the inner light of faith, that enables us to see beyond all the circumstances of our life to the very source of our existence, to God our Creator and our Father. All our existence, our very being, comes ultimately from God. As we pray in the Psalms:

> For it was you who formed my inward parts;
> you knit me together in my mother's womb.
> I praise you, for I am fearfully and wonderfully made.
>
> Psalm 139:13-14

By revealing to us that God is our loving Father, Jesus seeks to engage our hearts. He reveals the intimate and personal relationship each one of us has, or could have, with God. It is that personal relationship that the human heart yearns for. The question then is not "How do I think about God?", but "How do I relate to God?" How do I acknowledge that God is my Creator and that he loves me with an infinite love? It is in and through that loving relationship that we have access to God in our prayers.

The way of the heart

The way of the heart is different from the way of the head. In prayer, in our search for the presence of God in our life, we follow the way of the heart. As the seventeenth-century French philosopher Blaise Pascal said, "The heart has its reasons, of which reason knows nothing."[2] After years of searching to discover the meaning of his restlessness, St Augustine burst forth with this classic explanation:

> Too late have I loved you, O Beauty so ancient and so new,
> too late have I loved you. Behold, you were within me, while
> I was outside; it was there that I sought you, and, a deformed
> creature, rushed headlong upon these things of beauty which
> you have made. You were with me, but I was not with you.

---

2 Blaise Pascal, *Pensées* (Penguin Classics Ed.) (London: Penguin, 2003), 127.

> They kept me apart from you, those fair things which, if
> they were not in you, would not exist at all. You have called
> to me, and cried out, and have shattered my deafness.
> You blazed forth with light, and have shone upon me, and
> you have put blindness to flight. You have sent forth
> fragrance, and I have drawn my breath, and I pant after you.
> I have tasted you, and I hunger and thirst after you. You have
> touched me, and I have burned for your peace.[3]

Our Creator, like every good human father, wants us to be close to him and so he comes to make a home with us. God never abandons us or forsakes us. He accepts each one of us as his beloved daughter or son. And, of course, he expects us to acknowledge him and relate to him as our loving Father. But sometimes we can forget this loving care that God our Father has for us. As Augustine said, "You were with me, but I was not with you." We can be distracted by so many earthly things and forget about the presence of God within us. In his parable of the prodigal son, Jesus discusses this human weakness and how the Father responds to it:

> There was a man who had two sons. The younger of them
> said to his father, "Father, give me the share of the property
> that will belong to me." So he divided his property between
> them. A few days later the younger son gathered all he had
> and travelled to a distant country, and there he squandered
> his property in dissolute living.
>
> Luke 15:11-13

How is the story of that young man going to end? We can imagine those Pharisees, to whom Jesus was telling this parable, being filled with righteous indignation. They would not be surprised when the next scene describes how the young man runs out of money and meets with disaster. We read:

---

[3] St Augustine, *Confessions*, 10, 17.

> When he had spent everything, a severe famine took place throughout that country, and he began to be in need. So he went and hired himself out to one of the citizens of that country, who sent him to his fields to feed the pigs. He would gladly have filled himself with the pods the pigs were eating; and no one gave him anything.
>
> Luke 15:14-16

Down in the gutter

For the Pharisees to whom Jesus was telling his parable, pigs were unclean animals. Now that young man who had left his father's house and squandered his inheritance is mixing with pigs, feeding them and even longing to eat their very food. The prodigal's dream of a world of unrestrained freedom and pleasure in "a distant country" has now become his nightmare existence as a swineherd. How is he going to survive? The story begins to relate an inward journey:

> But when he came to himself he said, "How many of my father's hired hands have bread enough and to spare, but here I am dying of hunger! I will get up and go to my father, and I will say to him, 'Father, I have sinned against heaven and before you; I am no longer worthy to be called your son; treat me like one of your hired hands.'" So he set off and went to his father.
>
> Luke 15:17-20

The young spendthrift "came to himself". Pope Benedict XVI said that a better translation is "He went into himself".[4] In escaping from his homeland to that "distant country", he was really on the run from his true self, from his true homeland. Now in his destitution he begins to remember that he once had a different life when he was at home in his father's house. He is getting in touch with his human dignity, which he fears he has lost for ever by turning his back on God and on his father and living a life of debauchery. Pope Benedict XVI wrote:

---

4 Pope Benedict XVI, *Jesus of Nazareth, Vol. 1* (London: Bloomsbury, 2007), 204.

He is on a pilgrimage toward the truth of his existence, and that means "homeward." When the Church Fathers offer this "existential" exposition of the son's journey home, they are also explaining to us what "conversion" is, what sort of sufferings and inner purifications it involves, and we may safely say that they understood the essence of the parable correctly and help us to realize its relevance for today.[5]

The prodigal's self-esteem has hit rock bottom. Gone is the swaggering self-assurance that demanded his share of the estate. He will now be happy if his father merely hires him as one of his labourers. He will confess his sins to his father, acknowledge that he no longer deserves to be called his son and take on a new identity as a servant in his father's house. As Pope St John Paul II observed:

> He realizes that he no longer has any right except to be an employee in his father's house. His decision is taken in full consciousness of what he has deserved and of what he can still have a right to in accordance with the norms of justice. Precisely this reasoning demonstrates that, at the center of the prodigal's consciousness, the sense of lost dignity is emerging, the sense of that dignity that springs from the relationship of son with the father. And it is with this decision that he sets out.[6]

As Jesus prepares his audience for the return of the son to his father's house, all eyes will be fixed on the father. How will the father react when the son walks in to make his confession and look for a paid job? Will he keep him outside the door or will he invite him in? The father does neither. Jesus tells us what the father does in these words:

> While he was still far off, his father saw him and was filled with compassion; he ran and put his arms around him and kissed him. Then the son said to him, "Father, I have sinned

---
5 Ibid., 205.
6 Pope St John Paul II, *On the Mercy of God* (1980), paragraph 5.

against heaven and before you; I am no longer worthy to be called your son." But the father said to his slaves, "Quickly, bring out a robe – the best one – and put it on him; put a ring on his finger and sandals on his feet. And get the fatted calf and kill it, and let us eat and celebrate; for this son of mine was dead and is alive again; he was lost and is found!" And they began to celebrate.

Luke 15:20-24

What a dramatisation of the father's love and compassion! The Pharisees were criticising Jesus for "welcoming sinners and eating with them" (see Luke 15:2). Now those same Pharisees will have to judge the actions of the father. The prodigal felt that he had no right to be called his father's son, and the Pharisees would surely agree with that. But the father was fully aware that he had a right and a duty to be his son's father. And that surely challenges the Pharisees. The son's sins had certainly hurt his father, but beneath those sins the father sees the dignity and worth of his destitute son who is trying to find his way back to his father's house. The father is also aware that when the son departed from him, for the freedom of a distant land, he didn't cease to be a father and he didn't depart from his son. He had watched every day for his son's return. That is why he was able to see him "while he was still a long way off". As Pope Francis writes:

> The son was always in the father's heart, even though he had left him, even though he had squandered his whole inheritance, his freedom. The Father with patience, love, hope and mercy had never for a second stopped thinking about him, and as soon as he sees him still far off, he runs out to meet him and embrace him with tenderness, the tenderness of God, without a word of reproach: he has returned! And that is the joy of the Father. God is always waiting for us, he never grows tired.[7]

---

7   Pope Francis, *The Church of Mercy* (London: Darton, Longman and Todd, 2014), 3.

Love is transformed into mercy

The son on his return to his father's house discovers the depth of the father's love. The father had never rejected him but had watched each day for his return. Burdened with guilt, the son believed that there was no way back for him into the bosom of his family; he believed that his sins compelled his father to deprive him of his rights as a son; he discovered that while the father had lost his son, the son had never lost his father. The father of the prodigal, with his paternal embrace and kiss, forgives his prodigal son and receives him back into his home. The fact that he had lost his way and lived an immoral and reckless life, spending all his inheritance, could not dispossess him of his father's love. The father loved him, not because he was a good boy but because he was his son. With the dramatic manifestation of his love, the father begins to heal that famine of lost love in his son's heart, which robbed him of the sense of his dignity and worth as a human being and as the son of his father.

The father's right to be faithful to his paternal love for his son is manifested in his merciful welcome-home embrace, without judgement or demand for justice and restitution. There is no mention of either justice or restitution in the parable. Pope St John Paul II writes:

> Nevertheless, the relationship between justice and love, that is manifested as mercy, is inscribed with great exactness in the Gospel parable. It becomes more evident that love is transformed into mercy when it is necessary to go beyond the precise norm of justice – precise and often narrow.[8]

The father's love for his prodigal son knows no bounds. He commands his servants to serve his son, to respect him, to treat him with dignity and not to scorn him because of the disgrace he has brought upon the family. So the servants clothe the returning prodigal with the best robe – the sign of his restored dignity as son; they put a ring on his finger –

---
8 Pope St John Paul II, *On the Mercy of God* (1980), paragraph 5.

the sign of his restored authority as son; they put sandals on his feet – the sign that he is not a slave any more. And then the father calls for a celebration, a big feast, because "'this son of mine was dead and is alive again; he was lost and is found!' And they began to celebrate" (Luke 15:24).

Love certainly has been transformed into mercy. Now the father, his whole household and all his invited guests celebrate the return of his younger son, who had lost his way but has rediscovered it. He is the son in his father's house.

The elder son's rage

Filled with joy at his son's safe return to the family, the father has to face the refusal of his elder son to join in the celebration. The parable now presents the anger and resentment in the heart of the elder son:

> Now his elder son was in the field; and when he came and approached the house, he heard music and dancing. He called one of the slaves and asked what was going on. He replied, "Your brother has come, and your father has killed the fatted calf, because he has got him back safe and sound." Then he became angry and refused to go in.
>
> Luke 15:25-28

The joy of the father is once again turned into sadness by a son. How could his elder son not share in his joy at the safe return of his younger brother? So the father goes out to meet his elder son:

> He ... began to plead with him. But he answered his father, "Listen! For all these years I have been working like a slave for you, and I have never disobeyed your command; yet you have never given me even a young goat so that I might celebrate with my friends. But when this son of yours came back, who has devoured your property with prostitutes, you killed the fatted calf for him!"
>
> Luke 15:28-30

The elder son's deep resentment becomes apparent in his charge against his father: "All these years I have slaved for you, never disobeyed your orders, yet you never offered me so much as a kid for me to celebrate with my friends." He is speaking more like a hired man than like a son of the father. His father can only reply with a reassuring gentleness and love:

> "Son, you are always with me, and all that is mine is yours. But we had to celebrate and rejoice, because this brother of yours was dead and has come to life; he was lost and has been found."
>
> Luke 15:31-32

In his anger and resentment the elder son couldn't – or didn't want to – hear the father's words, "All I have is yours." What he wanted was for the father to dismiss the younger son and banish him from his home. He didn't want his sinful brother back in the house. He was acting like a Pharisee, and that is why Jesus told the Pharisees who were criticising him for welcoming and eating with sinners this parable of the prodigal son.

Being like the Father

Since God our Father, with his Son, Jesus Christ, makes a home in our hearts, we receive the grace from the Holy Spirit to imitate them in all our own relationships with family, friends and even enemies. Our heavenly Father is full of mercy and compassion and Jesus loves us so much that he laid down his life for our redemption. Our love for them in return involves loving all our sisters and brothers, whom they love. Speaking about loving our neighbours, Jesus says, "Love your enemies and pray for those who persecute you, so that you may be children of your Father in heaven. ... For if you love those who love you, what reward do you have? Do not even the tax-collectors do the same?" (Matthew 5:44-46). Jesus asks us to love friend and foe alike. Everyone we know, good or bad, is a brother or sister, and as God's children they have a place in our heart. With the friends who love us we can relax and enjoy their company; with those who, for whatever reason, treat us badly, we refrain from passing judgement and we pray for them. The hurt that a person who dislikes us can inflict on our heart can be healed only by our prayer of forgiveness. The more we hold on to the hurt, the bigger it becomes. As the Church prays Psalm 103 in the Divine Office, she proclaims how God deals with us poor sinners:

> Bless the Lord, O my soul,
> and all that is within me,
> bless his holy name.
> Bless the Lord, O my soul,
> and do not forget all his benefits –
> who forgives all your iniquity,
> who heals all your diseases,
> who redeems your life from the Pit,
> who crowns you with steadfast love and mercy,
> who satisfies you with good as long as you live
> so that your youth is renewed like the eagle's.
>
> Psalm 103:1-5

In that prayer we say, "[Let] all that is within me bless his holy name." That "all" includes not just the good and happy memories but also the bad and painful ones. The elder brother in the parable of the prodigal son obviously had painful memories. He refused to join his father in celebrating the return of his younger brother; he accused his father of not giving him "so much as a kid for me to celebrate with my friends". He was stuck in unforgivingness and was not yet willing to pray, "All that is within me bless his holy name", because he wanted to hold on to his painful memories.

Gratitude to God

As we ponder in our hearts the "love and mercy" of God our Father, we want to spontaneously say, "Bless the Lord, all that is within me." That prayer is a prayer of gratitude to God. Gratitude to God for his goodness, mercy and forgiveness should be our first response to God. True gratitude to God doesn't end with God but by its very nature is shared with everyone in our life who does us good, no matter how small. The Holy Spirit gives us the grace of gratitude in our hearts for those who do us good and the grace of forgiveness for those who treat us badly. The prodigal son's father was so grateful that his son had returned that he ran to welcome him home; he embraced him, kissed him and forgave him. The father knew that his lost son was a defeated and broken-hearted young man and he wanted to give him a big homecoming celebration to assure him of his welcome back to the family. Pope Francis expressed this well:

> The figure of the Father in the parable reveals the heart of God. He is the Merciful Father who, in Jesus, loves us beyond measure, always awaits our conversion every time we make mistakes; he awaits our return when we turn away from him thinking, we can do without him; he is always ready to open his arms no matter what happened. God also continues to consider us his children, even when we get lost, and comes to us with tenderness when we return to him. He addresses us so kindly when we believe we are right. The errors we commit, even if bad, do not wear out the fidelity of his love. In the Sacrament of Reconciliation, we can always start out anew: He welcomes us, gives us the dignity of being his children and tells us: "Go ahead! Be at peace! Rise, go ahead!"[9]

---

9   https://www.vatican.va/content/francesco/en/angelus/2016, 6 March.

God our Creator

God our Father is also our Creator. At the very beginning of the creation of human beings, God said, "Let us make humankind in our image, according to our likeness" (Genesis 1:26). Each of us was born in the likeness of God. When God created our first parents, Adam and Eve, he placed them in the beautiful Garden of Eden. It was in that garden that they were tempted by the serpent, the devil, and succumbed to the temptation. We call that the Original Sin. They were expelled from the Garden of Eden but they were not deprived of their likeness to God. God promised them a redeemer. He said to the serpent, "I will put enmity between you and the woman, and between your offspring and hers; he will strike your head, and you will strike his heel" (Genesis 3:15). These words are known as the Protoevangelium, the first Gospel, the promise of redemption. Sin had entered the world by the disobedience of our first parents. God promised them a redeemer, one who would put right what they had done wrong. In God's time our Redeemer, Jesus Christ, was born of the Virgin Mary through the power of the Holy Spirit. St John the Evangelist tells us the purpose of Christ's coming: "The Son of God was revealed for this purpose, to destroy the works of the devil" (1 John 3:8). The Son of God appeared on earth as the son of Mary. He came to proclaim the good news of God the Father's infinite love for us. By his death and resurrection, Jesus Christ won salvation for the whole human race.

When his disciples asked Jesus to teach them how to pray, he said:
>Pray then in this way:
>Our Father in heaven,
>hallowed be your name...
>Matthew 6:9

Jesus taught them and he teaches us the Lord's Prayer, the Our Father. Jesus is making it clear to us that, since our very life comes from God the Father, our prayers should, in the first place, be directed to the Father.

Our gratitude to God our Father

We begin all our prayers, or most of them, by making the sign of the cross and saying, "In the name of the Father and of the Son and of the Holy Spirit". And, as we say our prayers, whatever form they may take, we remind ourselves that we are not speaking to a God who is far away in a heaven beyond the stars but to the God who has made a home in our heart. To repeat the words of Jesus, "Those who love me will keep my word, and my Father will love them, and we will come to them and make our home with them" (John 14:23). Thanking God our Father with all our heart is our grateful response to that wonderful revelation Jesus gives us, when he makes known to us that God our Father comes with his Son, Jesus, to make a home in our sinful hearts. The infinite holiness of God – Father, Son and Holy Spirit – is within us as we open our hearts to make them welcome. And from within their home in our hearts Jesus says to us, "All things have been handed over to me by my Father; and no one knows the Son except the Father, and no one knows the Father except the Son and anyone to whom the Son chooses to reveal him" (Matthew 11:27).

Jesus has chosen to reveal the Father to us. It is not a physical revelation but a spiritual one. The Father is pure spirit. He is our teacher. Jesus says to us, "It is written in the prophets, 'And they shall all be taught by God.' Everyone who has heard and learned from the Father comes to me. Not that anyone has seen the Father except the one who is from God; he has seen the Father" (John 6:45-46).

While on this earth we do not see the Father with our physical eyes. But in our spiritual being we know the Father. He is our Creator; he sent his Son Jesus to redeem us from that Original Sin of our first parents and from our own sins; he has poured out his Spirit, the Holy Spirit, upon us. Each new day is a gift from the Father to us. As we contemplate the Father's great love for us, we say with St Paul:

Blessed be the God and Father of our Lord Jesus Christ, who has blessed us in Christ with every spiritual blessing in the heavenly places, just as he chose us in Christ before the foundation of the world to be holy and blameless before him in love. He destined us for adoption as his children through Jesus Christ, according to the good pleasure of his will, to the praise of his glorious grace that he freely bestowed on us in the Beloved.

Ephesians 1:3-6

Personal spiritual exercise for internalising the message of this chapter

- Centre yourself; sitting upright; breathing rhythmically; clearing your mind of all preoccupations.
- Bring yourself to bodily stillness.
- Jesus says, "The time is fulfilled, and the kingdom of God has come near; repent, and believe in the good news" (Mark 1:15). Now gratefully thank the Lord for his mercy and forgiveness.
- Experience the Father rushing to embrace you and welcome you.
- Be still for some time in the presence of the God of mercy and compassion, and receive his love.
- Now focus again on your breathing as you relax in God's presence.
- And bring yourself gently back to the world.

This spiritual exercise will deepen your awareness of being in the presence of the God of grace and show you how God has embraced you with his love and mercy.

CHAPTER THREE

JESUS, REMEMBER ME

When you are at home, you have easy-going conversations with family members or with friends who have dropped in for a chat. You talk about everything that is going on in the world and sometimes about what is going on in your own life. Home is where you feel secure. In the same way, when we are at home in Christ, we talk to him about everything that is going on in our own life. We call this prayer. But we don't do all the talking. Jesus has a lot that he wants to say to us and we have to listen to him. So our conversation at home in Jesus is one of talking and listening. This psalm describes it well:

> Let me hear what God the Lord will speak,
> for he will speak peace to his people,
> to his faithful, to those who turn to him in their hearts.
>
> Psalm 85:8

When we are at home with Christ, we can relax in his peace, turn to him in our hearts and listen to what he says to us. But to hear his voice we have to be still. We cannot be doing all the talking or allowing all our worries, anxieties or fears to control our thoughts. We seek to do what the psalm says: "Be still, and know that I am God!" (Psalm 46:10). God is present in our heart. In stillness we enter our heart to give our Lord adoration, praise and thanksgiving. Now we can place all our worries, fears and doubts into Christ's hands. He has invited us to make our home with him and he will take good care of us.

The good thief on Calvary

God is our Father, and like every good father he will only give us what is truly good for us. Sometimes in our prayers, we can unconsciously be asking for something that seems good to us, at the time, but would not be good for our life. The fact that God sometimes doesn't give us what we are praying for is not a sign that he doesn't care for us. Rather, it is the proof that God loves us so much that he cannot give us something that would be bad for us. St Luke's story of the good thief is helpful. Two thieves were crucified alongside Jesus. Luke writes:

> One of the criminals who were hanged there kept deriding him and saying, "Are you not the Messiah? Save yourself and us!" But the other rebuked him, saying, "Do you not fear God, since you are under the same sentence of condemnation? And we indeed have been condemned justly, for we are getting what we deserved for our deeds, but this man has done nothing wrong." Then he said, "Jesus, remember me when you come into your kingdom." He replied, "Truly I tell you, today you will be with me in Paradise."
>
> Luke 23:39-43

Jesus himself promised salvation to that man who turned to him in his heart and asked just to be remembered. That is the power of God's gift of prayer from the heart. Jesus himself guarantees the good response to prayer when he says, "Ask, and it will be given to you; search, and you will find; knock, and the door will be opened for you" (Matthew 7:7). God will always grant what is best for our life of Christian witness and service. James bluntly gives us the reason that we sometimes don't get what we are praying for: "You do not have, because you do not ask. You ask and do not receive, because you ask wrongly, in order to spend what you get on your pleasures" (James 4:2-3).

The divine invitation

Accepting Christ's invitation to make our home in him opens the door to a new life with him. When St Paul had the opportunity to announce the good news of Christ to the pagan citizens of Athens, the cultural capital of the Roman Empire at the time, he summed up his message about the God that he worshipped by saying, "For 'In him we live and move and have our being'; as even some of your own poets have said, 'For we too are his offspring'" (Acts 17:28). Living in the faith that our life is God's gift and that we live in God is why Jesus can now invite us to make our home in him. He is our Redeemer and our God. He is also our brother. As the Second Vatican Council said, "By his incarnation, he, the Son of God, has in a certain way united himself with each individual."[1] There is no human being born into this world who does not have Jesus Christ as a brother. Billions of them, of course, have never had faith in Jesus or even heard of him, but he knows each one of them and he loves each one of them because he came to save each one of them. We have been blessed with the gift of faith in Jesus. We were baptised into Christ and became his body, his mystical body, members of his Church. This is the work of the Holy Spirit.

The Vatican Council, of course, is basing its teaching on what St Paul wrote in his letter to the Romans: "For as in one body we have many members, and not all the members have the same function, so we, who are many, are one body in Christ, and individually we are members one of another" (Romans 12:4-5).

---

1 Second Vatican Council, *Constitution on the Church in the Modern World*, 22.

The gift of prayer

To make our life in Jesus peaceful and grateful, God gives us the gift of prayer. There are many different kinds of prayer: we can just be still with Christ and listen, or we can talk to him about everything that is going on in our life; we can say the prayers of the Psalms in the Divine Office or we can pray the rosary in honour of our Blessed Mother; we go to holy Mass, the great prayer of the Eucharist, or we can make visits to the Blessed Sacrament; we can contemplate the word of God in the sacred scriptures. Whatever form of prayer we use, we offer it to God in and through Christ. As members of Christ's body, each one of us represents that body when we come into God's presence to pray. Not only that, the whole body of Christ stands with us as we pray. This body of Christ, of which you are a member, includes all your family, all your friends, and also all those who are not friends and may even be enemies. So it is not just you, as a single individual, who has come into God's presence. You bring, as it were, the whole Church with you. Because you are in Christ and Christ is the Head, it is Christ himself who is with you every time you come into the presence of God the Father. It is in Christ and through Christ that you have access to the Father. In a beautiful sermon, St Augustine put it this way:

> God could give no greater gift to men and women than to make his Word, through whom he created all things, their head and to join them to him as his members, so that the Word might be both Son of God and son of man, one God with the Father, and one man with all men and women. The result is that when we speak to God in prayer we do not separate the Son from him, and when the body of the Son prays it does not separate its head from itself: it is one Saviour of his body, one Lord Jesus Christ, the Son of God, who prays for us and in us and is himself the object of our prayer. Christ prays for us as our priest, he prays in us as our head, he is the object of our prayers as our God.[2]

---

2 St Augustine, *Divine Office of Readings*, Wednesday of fifth week of Lent.

When you make your home in Christ, he prays for everyone in your life, which means he will be praying for your friends and foes alike. He came to redeem each one of them. He teaches us how to relate to those who don't relate well to us when he says, "I say to you that listen, Love your enemies, do good to those who hate you, bless those who curse you, pray for those who abuse you. ... If you love those who love you, what credit is that to you? For even sinners love those who love them" (Luke 6:27-28, 32). Christ is teaching us how to be at peace as we make our home in him. Many otherwise good people can hold on to their grudges, keep their hearts hardened towards their "enemies" and never think of praying for them. Then they are surprised that they lack inner peace in their own life and sometimes find it hard to make their home in Christ. Inner peace is Christ's gift as we forgive from the heart all those who treat us badly. Jesus shows us how to reclaim our inner peace: "Do not judge, and you will not be judged; do not condemn, and you will not be condemned. Forgive, and you will be forgiven" (Luke 6:37). If we accept these divine principles that Jesus teaches us at home in him, we will experience deep inner healing and peace. If, on the other hand, we hold on to judging, condemning and being unforgiving in our attitude, we will block the peace that Christ has for us. The apostle John makes this very clear: "By this we may be sure that we are in him: whoever says, 'I abide in him', ought to walk just as he walked" (1 John 2:5-6). As we make our home in Christ, we will experience deep inner healing and peace and we will have the inner strength to "walk as Jesus walked", to love and forgive our critics and to pray for them.

Enriching our whole life

Accepting Christ's invitation to make our home in him enriches our whole life, especially our prayer life. In Christ we will begin to do as Jesus recommends in St Luke's Gospel: "Then Jesus told them a parable about their need to pray always and not to lose heart" (Luke 18:1). Prayer is the oxygen of our spiritual life. It is our spiritual lifeline. Jesus will teach us how to pray always when we make our home in him. The essence of our prayer is in our loving relationship with God. God is our Father and Creator, who loves us with an everlasting love. Jesus, the Son of God, was sent by the Father to live among us as our brother. He was born of the Virgin Mary by the power of the Holy Spirit. He came among us to make the mercy and forgiveness of God his Father known to us. As our brother and our Redeemer, Jesus Christ is the revelation of God the Father. He knew that he would have to leave us by his death on the cross, but before he left his disciples, he promised them the gift of the Holy Spirit: "If you love me, you will keep my commandments. And I will ask the Father, and he will give you another Advocate, to be with you for ever. This is the Spirit of truth, whom the world cannot receive, because it neither sees him nor knows him. You know him, because he abides with you, and he will be in you" (John 14:15-17). What a life-giving promise! God's Holy Spirit is in each one of us who makes our home in Christ.

Meditating on the humanity and divinity of Christ

Christ's invitation to make our home in him entails meditating on both the humanity and the divinity of Jesus. The Son of God became a human being and was born of the Virgin Mary by the power of the Holy Spirit so that we, sinful human beings, could share in his divine nature as he now shares in our human nature. At every Mass we pray, "By the mystery of this water and wine may we share in the divinity of Christ who humbled himself to share in our humanity." It is not, of course, in Christ's physical body that we make our home but in his resurrected, glorified body. Our abiding in Christ is the mystery of our faith. Our brother Christ, Mary's son, is also the divine Son of God, infinite in power and glory. We do not know how to make our home in him, but once we accept his invitation, he will teach us. Through his Holy Spirit he will enlighten our minds; he will purify our hearts; he will guarantee that when death comes, we will rise with him from the dead; he will take away all fear of death and fill us with peace. It is through our life of prayer and good works that we can enter into these profound, divine mysteries. The Second Vatican Council taught this very consoling doctrine:

> Since Christ died for everyone, and since all are in fact called to one and the same destiny, which is divine, we must hold that the Holy Spirit offers to all the possibility of being made partners, in a way known to God, in the paschal mystery.[3]

The mystery of God's infinite love for each human being born into this world is beyond our comprehension. Not everyone shares our Christian faith but we believe that God gives to each person the opportunity of receiving eternal life. As St Paul wrote, "God wants everyone to be saved and reach full knowledge of the truth" (1 Timothy 2:4, NJB). Writing to the Romans, St Paul said, "God shows no partiality" (Romans 2:11). Christians are not God's favourites. God has given us the light of faith and through that faith we believe that we are God's sons and daughters. That is why we have the right to come into God's presence, speak to him in prayer, ask him for all that we need and pray for the whole human race. God loves equally those who, as yet, do not believe in Christ and those who do. Jesus said, "All things have been handed over to me by my Father; and no one knows the Son except the Father, and no one knows the Father except the Son and anyone to whom the Son chooses to reveal him" (Matthew 11:27). The very fact that we believe in God our Father means that Jesus has given us that revelation in our heart.

---

3 Second Vatican Council, *Gaudium et Spes* (The Pastoral Constitution on the Church in the Modern World, 1965), 22.

He has given us the light of faith. It is in and through that light of faith that we find our way into the presence of God in prayer. Jesus knows all those who don't yet know him and so he tells us, "I am the good shepherd. I know my own and my own know me... I lay down my life for the sheep. I have other sheep that do not belong to this fold. I must bring them also, and they will listen to my voice. So there will be one flock, one shepherd" (John 10:14-16). Christ came to redeem the whole human race. He has blessed us with faith so that we can now be his witnesses in the world and, as his evangelists, make him known to others. We don't keep the gift of faith for ourselves. We have to share it with others.

One body with Christ

When we make our home in Christ, we begin to remember that we are one body with Christ. As St Paul says, "For as in one body we have many members, and not all the members have the same function, so we, who are many, are one body in Christ, and individually we are members one of another" (Romans 12:4-5). We begin to realise more deeply that we are the body of Christ in the world, the "mystical body" of Christ our Saviour. We are, therefore, never alone when we come into the presence of God in prayer. Since we are members of Christ's body, we bring with us the whole body. That is why we begin the Lord's Prayer by saying "Our Father" and not "My Father" and "forgive us" not "forgive me". And when we say the Hail Mary we say, "Pray for us sinners" not "Pray for me, a sinner." As we make our home in Christ, we begin to realise that Jesus loves each human being equally and that each person is an honoured guest in his home. In his wonderful prayer to the Father at the Last Supper with his twelve apostles, Jesus said, "I ask not only on behalf of these, but also on behalf of those who will believe in me through their word, that they may all be one. As you, Father, are in me and I am in you, may they also be in us, so that the world may believe that you have sent me" (John 17:20-21). "May they be in us" – that is Christ's request as he prayed to the Father at his Last Supper with his disciples. He wants us to find our unity as his disciples, as his mystical body on earth, through our union with him and his heavenly Father. If we are not in union with our sisters and brothers on earth, if we do not love them as Christ loves us, it means we are not in union with Jesus and God our Father. We are in need of conversion and repentance before we can be at ease at home with Jesus. We recall again what Jesus says to us: "Those who love me will keep my word, and my Father will love them, and we will come to them and make our home with them" (John 14:23). The one rule for spiritual progress is "start again". The Lord never forsakes us. The fact that we become aware that we can slip up, take a wrong turn, forget about being members of Christ's body on earth, means that the Holy Spirit is at work in our hearts, inviting us to start again. We don't allow our failures to cancel the invitation to make our home in Christ. In God's presence we are always his family. Because we are members of Christ's body on earth, the whole Christ is present when we come before God our Father in prayer. St Paul tells us that "[Christ] is the head of the body, the church" (Colossians 1:18). That means that wherever we are, we are there as the members of God's family, the Church, which is Christ's body on earth.

Cultivating the awareness that Christians are Christ's body in the world inspires us to turn to the Holy Spirit, who is, as we say in our Creed at Mass, "the Lord, the giver of life". God has sent the Holy Spirit into our hearts to purify us from every stain of sin, to enlighten our minds, and to fill our hearts with the peace of Christ. Preparing our hearts to be at home in Christ involves a deep conversion of the heart, a true repentance for all our sins and a commitment to follow Jesus and walk in his ways. It is the Holy Spirit who gives us all these graces. As the priest says in the formula of Absolution: "He has sent the Holy Spirit among us for the forgiveness of our sins." Without the gentle action of the Holy Spirit, none of us would be able to turn our backs on sin. It is the Holy Spirit who teaches us how to pray. When we cross the threshold of prayer, we are consciously seeking to enter into the presence of God. That threshold is not in some holy place far away and outside ourselves, but within our own heart. God is closer to us than we are to ourselves. When Moses approached the burning bush, he was told, "Remove the sandals from your feet, for the place on which you are standing is holy ground" (Exodus 3:5). We are on holy ground when we enter the presence of God. We do so with reverence. As you turn to God in prayer in your living room or in your bedroom, you turn off the TV or the radio, you enter into the presence of God, and your living room or bedroom becomes holy ground. You become aware that God is with you. Of course, God is always with you, even when you are totally unaware of his presence, but once you become aware of his presence with you, your very surroundings take on a new meaning. You realise that you are on holy ground and that your home has become holy. You can now see it as the place where God dwells. Now your prayer time at home becomes very significant and very important. Your home becomes the house of God, where you and your family and all your friends can be at peace in God's presence, in Christ's presence.

Pondering in our heart

As we are preparing to make our home in Christ, our life of prayer takes on a new significance. We are opening our hearts to welcome God our Father and his Son, Jesus Christ, into our hearts and at the same time we are being welcomed by Jesus into his home. These are profound mysteries. How can we hold on to them? Our Blessed Lady shows us the way. St Luke tells us how she came to terms with the mysteries of her son's conception and birth with these words: "Mary treasured all these words and pondered them in her heart"

(Luke 2:19). It was not in her mind that Our Lady was pondering the mysteries that had been revealed to her, but in her heart. We can learn from Our Lady how to ponder and contemplate the great mystery of God's presence in our lives. We have to be still. As the psalm says, "Be still, and know that I am God!" (Psalm 46:10). When we come into God's presence, we have many requests to make to God but we should always try to have that moment of stillness and wait on the Lord. As the psalm says, "I waited patiently for the Lord; he inclined to me and heard my cry" (Psalm 40:1). It is in stillness in God's presence that we will get an answer to our prayers. As we try to be still, we will often be beset by all kinds of distractions. Don't let them discourage you in your pursuit of stillness. Just remind yourself that you are in God's presence, in stillness waiting on the Lord. Say a silent, favourite prayer, such as "Into your hands, O Lord, I commend my spirit", and then continue your moment of stillness in God's presence. In that stillness, ponder, as Our Lady did, the goodness and love of God in your heart.

God always hears our prayer. He will answer our prayer in his time. As we place all our trust in the Lord, we will gain inner peace. We cannot live a spiritual life without the basic spiritual nourishment that prayer provides. St Alphonsus Liguori put it this way:

> As moisture is necessary for the life of plants to prevent them from drying up, so, says St Chrysostom, is prayer necessary for our salvation. Prayer vivifies the soul, as the soul vivifies the body... Prayer is also called the food of the soul, because the body cannot be supported without food; nor can the soul, says St. Augustine, be kept alive without prayer: "As the flesh is nourished by food, so is man supported by prayers." All these comparisons used by the holy Fathers are intended by them to teach the absolute necessity of prayer for the salvation of everyone.[4]

---
4   St Alphonsus Liguori, *Prayer: The Great Means of Salvation and of Perfection* (Edmond, OK: Veritatis Publications, 2012, edited by Paul A. Boer, Sr), 10.

Because prayer is so important for our spiritual well-being, Jesus encourages us to make prayer a priority in our daily schedule with these words:

> So I say to you, Ask, and it will be given to you; search, and you will find; knock, and the door will be opened for you. For everyone who asks receives, and everyone who searches finds, and for everyone who knocks, the door will be opened. Is there anyone among you who, if your child asks for a fish, will give a snake instead of a fish? Or if the child asks for an egg, will give a scorpion? If you then, who are evil, know how to give good gifts to your children, how much more will the heavenly Father give the Holy Spirit to those who ask him!
>
> Luke 11:9-13

The Holy Spirit is the gift that God the Father always wants to give to each of us. The more we seek to make our home in Christ, the more Christ our Lord will fill us afresh with the Holy Spirit. We receive this grace and presence of the Spirit when we humbly ask God to pour out his Spirit in our lives. In the next chapter we will reflect on the gift of the Holy Spirit.

Personal spiritual exercise for internalising the message of this chapter

- Centre yourself; sitting upright; breathing rhythmically; clearing your mind of all preoccupations.
- Bring yourself to bodily stillness.
- The priest prays at the Offertory of the Mass, "By the mystery of this water and wine may we come to share in the divinity of Christ who humbled himself to share in our humanity."
- Silently in your heart make that request to share in the divinity of Christ each time you are at Mass.
- Now focus again on your breathing as you relax in God's presence.
- And bring yourself gently back to the world.

This spiritual exercise will deepen your awareness of being in the presence of the God of grace and show you how God has embraced you with his love and mercy.

CHAPTER FOUR

THE GIFT OF THE HOLY SPIRIT

At the Last Supper with his disciples Jesus said, "I tell you the truth: it is to your advantage that I go away, for if I do not go away the Advocate will not come to you; but if I go, I will send him to you" (John 16:7). The disciples would have been shocked by Jesus' saying "It is to your advantage that I go away". They had committed their lives to being with Jesus: they were witnesses to the great miracles he worked; they were encouraged by his new and creative teaching; they enjoyed his friendship. What could be better for them than to have Jesus with them always? Yet Jesus is saying that his leaving them will be to their advantage because his place will be taken by the Holy Spirit, the Spirit of truth.

Who is this Spirit of truth? That question would have been in the minds of those first disciples. And that same question is in the minds of every generation of Christians. Jesus said to his disciples:

> I still have many things to say to you, but you cannot bear them now. When the Spirit of truth comes, he will guide you into all the truth; for he will not speak on his own, but will speak whatever he hears, and he will declare to you the things that are to come. He will glorify me, because he will take what is mine and declare it to you. All that the Father has is mine. For this reason I said that he will take what is mine and declare it to you.
>
> John 16:12-15

As we prayerfully begin to explore the gift of the Holy Spirit, the presence of the Holy Spirit in our hearts, that same Spirit will guide us into the full truth.

When the angel Gabriel visited the Blessed Virgin Mary with the news that she was to bear a son and call him Jesus, Mary had a question for Gabriel: "How can this be, since I am a virgin?" The angel responded, "The Holy Spirit will come upon you, and the power of the Most High will overshadow you; therefore the child to be born will be holy; he will be called Son of God." In response to Gabriel's clarification Mary said, "Here am I, the servant of the Lord; let it be with me according to your word" (Luke 1:34-38). Mary obviously knew who the Holy Spirit was. She knew that the Holy Spirit was "the Lord, the giver of life", as we say in the Creed. She also knew that it would be through the power of the Holy Spirit that she would give birth to the Son of God. Mary was filled with the Holy Spirit from the moment of her birth. That is why she could speak those marvellous words to the angel Gabriel: "Here am I, the servant of the Lord."

The Holy Spirit in the life and ministry of Jesus

Before Jesus began his mission of proclaiming the good news of God's mercy, he went to the Jordan river to be baptised by John the Baptist. When he came out of the water and was praying, the heaven was opened, and the Holy Spirit descended on him in bodily form like a dove and a voice came from heaven: "You are my Son, the Beloved; with you I am well pleased" (Luke 3:21-22). St Luke then tells us that "Jesus, full of the Holy Spirit, returned from the Jordan and was led by the Spirit in the wilderness, where for forty days he was tempted by the devil" (Luke 4:1-2). After his forty days in the wilderness, Luke tells us, "Then Jesus, filled with the power of the Spirit, returned to Galilee, and a report about him spread through all the surrounding country" (Luke 4:14). Jesus began his mission in the power of the Holy Spirit. His preaching, his miracles of healing, the time he gave to teaching his apostles: all these works were done through the power of the Holy Spirit. And Jesus said to his apostles, "You will receive power when the Holy Spirit has come upon you; and you will be my witnesses in Jerusalem, in all Judea and Samaria, and to the ends of the earth" (Acts 1:8). The Holy Spirit was with Jesus throughout his ministry and now the Holy Spirit is with us as we follow Jesus today. We have to listen to the Spirit. Jesus makes this very clear when he says to us, "I still have many things to say to you, but you cannot bear them now. When the Spirit of truth comes, he will guide you into all the truth" (John 16:12-13). In every new generation in the Church, the Holy Spirit is guiding God's people. Jesus says to us, "The Advocate, the Holy Spirit, whom the Father will send in my name, will teach you everything, and remind you of all that I have said to you. Peace I leave with you; my peace I give to you" (John 14:26-27).

The Holy Spirit continues to guide Christ's Church today. That is why the members of the Church are encouraged to listen to the Spirit. Each member of the Church received the outpouring of the Holy Spirit at their baptism and again at their confirmation. The Holy Spirit remains active, though invisible, throughout their whole life. The more they get to know the Spirit during their life, the more they will be able to become a true disciple of Christ. As the psalm says, "Let me hear what God the Lord will speak, for he will speak peace to his people, to his faithful, to those who turn to him in their hearts" (Psalm 85:8). Throughout the history of our Church, we have been encouraged by all the great saints to pray daily to the Holy Spirit and ask for his guidance. This is one of those prayers that has been handed on to us:

> Come Holy Spirit, fill the hearts of your faithful and kindle
> in them the fire of your love. Send forth your Spirit and they
> shall be created, and you shall renew the face of the earth.
> O God, who by the light of the Holy Spirit, did instruct the
> hearts of the faithful, grant that by the same Holy Spirit
> we may be truly wise and ever enjoy His consolations,
> Through Christ Our Lord, Amen.

The first line of this prayer dates back to the twelfth century.

Christ's faithful have always been moved to express devotion to the Holy Spirit in their prayer life. Our devotion to the Holy Spirit brings us into a relationship with the Spirit. We begin to know the Spirit and place all our trust in him.

St Paul was the great teacher of the presence of the Holy Spirit in our hearts. Writing to the Christians in Rome, he said, "If the Spirit of him who raised Jesus from the dead dwells in you, he who raised Christ from the dead will give life to your mortal bodies also through his Spirit that dwells in you" (Romans 8:11). In our Creed at Sunday Mass, we confess our faith in the Spirit's presence within us when we say, "I believe in the Holy Spirit, the Lord, the giver of life." The Holy Spirit who raised Christ from the dead now dwells in us. He is our spiritual life-giver. He will also raise us from the dead on the Last Day. In this life the Spirit dwells within us as our sanctifier and our teacher, our guardian and our protector.

Jesus said to Nicodemus, "Very truly, I tell you, no one can enter the kingdom of God without being born of water and Spirit" (John 3:5). In God's plan for his people, the Holy Spirit is at the centre of our Christian life. We need to remember that God had made this great promise to his people in the Old Testament: "I will sprinkle clean water upon you, and you shall be clean from all your uncleannesses, and from all your idols I will cleanse you. A new heart I will give you, and a new spirit I will put within you; and I will remove from your body the heart of stone and give you a heart of flesh. I will put my spirit within you" (Ezekiel 36:25-27). God fulfilled that promise in us on the day of our baptism. We were born again, through our baptism, as a son or daughter of God by the power of the Holy Spirit. The word of the Lord now echoes in our heart: "O that today you would listen to his voice! Do not harden your hearts" (Psalm 95:7-8). As the newborn sons and daughters of God, we listen to God's word and we live by it. Jesus said in his response to the devil's temptation in the wilderness, "One does not live by bread alone, but by every word that comes from the mouth of God" (Matthew 4:4).

Living by the word of God

We were created by the Word of God and God invites us to live by his word. Pope Benedict XVI highlighted this truth in his famous *Exhortation on the Word of God*, where he writes:

> We were created in the word and we live in the word; we cannot understand ourselves unless we are open to this dialogue. The word of God discloses the filial and relational nature of human existence… In this dialogue with God we come to understand ourselves and we discover an answer to our heart's deepest question.[1]

Because each of us has been created by the Word of God, it is necessary for us to begin to see ourselves as God sees us. To do that we must enter into a dialogue with God. We know that we are weak and sinful, but we also believe in faith that God has redeemed us, that Christ died for our sins and that he poured out on us the gift of the Holy Spirit. We believe that the Holy Spirit who resides in our inner self is with us always. We can only understand ourselves and the meaning and purpose of our life when we are in dialogue with God our Father who created us, with God the Son, our Lord Jesus Christ, who redeemed us, and with the Holy Spirit, who is "the Lord, the giver of life". Pope Benedict XVI has a necessary recommendation for each of us:

> It is decisive to present the word of God in its capacity to enter into dialogue with the everyday problems which people face. We need to make every effort to share the word of God as an openness to our problems, a response to our questions, a broadening of our values and the fulfilment of our aspirations.[2]

---

1 Pope Benedict XVI, *Verbum Domini: post-synodal exhortation on the word of God* (2010), 22/23.
2 Pope Benedict XVI, *Verbum Domini*, 22.

We have to keep reminding ourselves of Jesus' statement that we "[do not] live by bread alone, but by every word that comes from the mouth of God" (Matthew 4:4). The word that God speaks to us each day is a life-giving word. It would be a sad ending to our day if we never listened to God's word, thanked him for his promises, asked for his mercy and forgiveness, and promised our Lord Jesus that we would do our best to live by God's word from now on. We need then to entrust all our weaknesses, all our sinfulness, all our failures, all our restlessness to our Lord Jesus and make our home in him as he invites us to do. Then we will be able to have a life-changing dialogue with God, the Father, Son and Holy Spirit, who dwells within us. God knows that we cannot enter into peace if we are not in union with him. The Lord Jesus says, "The Advocate, the Holy Spirit, whom the Father will send in my name, will teach you everything and remind you of all that I have said to you. Peace I leave with you; my peace I give to you. I do not give to you as the world gives. Do not let your hearts be troubled, and do not let them be afraid" (John 14:26-27).

Jesus makes clear to us the teaching role of the Holy Spirit: He "will teach you everything". That clarifies the role of the Holy Spirit in our lives – he is our teacher: we listen to him because, as Jesus says, "he will remind you of all I have said to you". Jesus also makes it plain that it is God the Father who sends us the Spirit. But we have to ponder well what he says: "The Advocate, the Holy Spirit, whom the Father will send in my name." The Holy Spirit is sent to us *in Jesus' name.* Jesus is making it very clear to us that the Holy Trinity, Father, Son and Holy Spirit, are fully involved in the work of our redemption. God our Father who created us sent his Son, Jesus, born of the Virgin Mary, to redeem us and then sent, in Jesus' name, the Holy Spirit to be our teacher, who will remind us of everything Jesus said to us while he was on this earth. St Paul emphasised this truth to the Corinthians when he wrote, "No one can say 'Jesus is Lord' except by the Holy Spirit" (1 Corinthians 12:3).

The Holy Spirit is the New Covenant

At the Last Supper, Christ proclaimed the New Covenant between God and us with the words: "This cup that is poured out for you is the new covenant in my blood" (Luke 22:20). The sacrifice of his life on the cross, which he offered to the Father for our sake, reconciled us with God and gained for us a New Covenant, a new and personal relationship with God our Father. What is the New Covenant? One of the greatest theologians, St Thomas Aquinas, writing in the thirteenth century, said, "The New Covenant consists in the inpouring of the Holy Spirit."[3] In another commentary St Thomas wrote, "As the Holy Spirit works in us charity which is the fullness of the Law, he himself is the New Covenant."[4]

When we talk, then, about the New Covenant, we are speaking about the outpouring of the Spirit on us and on all those who turn to Christ in prayer and accept him as their Saviour. The New Covenant is not an external legal contract between God and us. It is the very presence of the Holy Spirit in our hearts, a presence that can only be recognised with faith. We have been sanctified and purified by our infilling with the Holy Spirit. And, if we lose our spiritual balance and fall away, the moment we cry out to the Holy Spirit for help we will receive it. The thief whom we call the "good" thief said on Calvary, "Jesus, remember me when you come into your kingdom" and Jesus replied, "Truly I tell you, today you will be with me in Paradise" (Luke 23:42-43).

Pope St John Paul II, in his book *The Spirit: the giver of life and love*, wrote, "The Holy Spirit, one in being with the Father and the Son, remains the 'hidden God.' While operating in the Church and in the world, he is not manifested visibly, unlike the Son."[5] We don't see the Holy Spirit. When Christ fulfilled his promise and sent the Holy Spirit on his disciples, they began to understand why it was better for

---

3 St Thomas Aquinas, Heb. Cap. 8. lect. 2.
4 St Thomas Aquinas, in 2 Cor. Cap. 3, lect. 2.
5 Pope St John Paul II, *The Spirit: the giver of life and love* (Boston, MA: Pauline Books and Media, 1996), 46.

them personally that Jesus had gone away. The invisible presence of the Holy Spirit in their hearts and minds and in their community meant that Christ was with them now in a new way and they were with him in a new way.

What difference does the Holy Spirit make in our lives?

It is very helpful and indeed very necessary for us to become aware of and reflect on this invisible, abiding presence of the Holy Spirit at work in the Church, in the world and in our hearts. The Spirit is the active memory of the Church; he is the teacher of our faith. As the new *Catechism* says, "By his transforming power, he makes the mystery of Christ present here and now."[6] The Spirit is in the good works and the witness of Christians all over the world as they seek to live out the life of Christ; when we pray, it is the Spirit who prays in our hearts. The Orthodox Patriarch Ignatius of Latakia in Syria said in his 1968 address to the World Council of Churches:

Without the Holy Spirit:

God is far away,
Christ stays in the past,
the gospel is a dead letter,
the Church simply an organization,
authority a matter of domination,
mission a matter of propaganda,
liturgy is no more than an evocation,
Christian living a slave morality.

---

6 *The Catechism of the Catholic Church* (second edition), 1092.

But with the Holy Spirit:

>the cosmos is resurrected and groans
>with the birth-pangs of the Kingdom,
>the risen Christ is there,
>the Gospel is the power of life,
>the Church shows forth the life of the Trinity,
>authority is a liberating service,
>mission is a Pentecost,
>the liturgy is both memorial and anticipation,
>human action is deified.[7]

With Bishop Ignatius' clear teaching on the difference that the Holy Spirit makes in our lives, we will begin to understand more clearly what Jesus meant when he said, "It is to your advantage that I go away, for if I do not go away, the Advocate will not come to you; but if I go, I will send him to you" (John 16:6-7). We can now see how the Holy Spirit is invisibly at work in our family and in our heart each time we turn to God in prayer. In fact, we can turn to God in prayer only because the Spirit is *already* in our heart.

The answer to all the materialism of our age

Pope St John Paul II, in his first encyclical letter to the Church, called us all to reflect more deeply on the gift of the Holy Spirit, which makes us one with Christ and alive in Christ. He wrote:

> The present-day Church seems to repeat with ever greater fervour and with holy insistence: "Come, Holy Spirit!" Come! Come! This appeal to the Spirit, intended precisely to obtain the Spirit, is the answer to all the 'materialisms' of our age.[8]

---

7   Ignatius of Latakia, Meditation at the Fourth World Assembly of Churches, July 1968, published in *The Uppsala Report* (Geneva, 1969), 298; cited in Rupert Shortt, *God is No Thing* (London: Hurst and Company, 2016), 67.
8   Pope St John Paul II, *Redemptor Hominis* ("The Redeemer of Man"), 18.

St John Paul's teaching that the appeal to the Spirit "is the answer to all the 'materialisms' of our age" is surely a word of encouragement that we should listen to afresh every day. It is very easy to lapse into discouragement over the Church and over our society. Many things have gone wrong in our Church: great scandals regarding the behaviour of some clergy have disturbed and upset the faithful of all ages; we are very aware that vocations to the priesthood and the religious life in Britain and Ireland have decreased dramatically; we are acutely aware that many of our young people do not join the parish community for Sunday Mass; family life is being challenged and undermined in many ways; and, with so much malevolence and violence in our world today, our societies have become much less peaceful and safe. Fresh encouragement is needed to face all these challenges. We can find that encouragement in Pope St John Paul II's words: "The appeal to the Spirit is the answer to all the 'materialisms' of our age." We have the answer to hand. We can invoke the Holy Spirit each day to come afresh on the Church, on our family, on our society and on ourselves. The Holy Spirit, as we say in the Creed, "is the Lord, the giver of life". As we ask the Spirit to come, he will give new life and new hope to us and to the Church. St Paul prayed this prayer for hope through the Spirit in his letter to the Romans: "May the God of hope fill you with all joy and peace in believing, so that you may abound in hope by the power of the Holy Spirit" (Romans 15:13). To be rich in hope is the gift of the Holy Spirit, a gift that we need every day.

Through the presence of the Holy Spirit in our hearts, we believe that we are now in union with Christ. We are the body of Christ. As St Paul preached so constantly, "Now you together are Christ's body, and each of you is a different part of it" (1 Corinthians 12:27, my paraphrase). It is through the presence of the Holy Spirit in our hearts that we can now believe that Christ, with his heavenly Father, dwells in us. The presence of the Holy Spirit in our hearts makes us a sacramental people.

Sacrament

A sacrament is a visible sign of invisible grace. We see the visible sign with our physical eyes. But it is with the "eye of faith" that we see the invisible grace of the Holy Spirit present in the sacrament of the New Covenant and being communicated to us. For instance, the pouring of water over the head of the person being baptised, with the words "I baptise you in the name of the Father and of the Son and of the Holy Spirit", is the visible sign that we see at a baptism. The invisible grace of the person being filled with the Holy Spirit, "being born of water and Spirit" (John 3:5), can be seen only "with the eye of faith". We believe that God's redeeming love comes to us in that visible sign. The visible sign in the celebration of the sacrament of reconciliation is the penitent kneeling or sitting with the priest, asking for a blessing and then simply confessing whatever sins are troubling his or her conscience at that moment, and the priest pronouncing these words of absolution: "I absolve you from all your sins in the name of the Father and of the Son and of the Holy Spirit." We are blessed with the living word of God and we seek to live our lives according to it. In his second letter to the Corinthians St Paul wrote, "You yourselves are our letter, written on our hearts, to be known and read by all; and you show that you are a letter of Christ, prepared by us, written not with ink but with the Spirit of the living God, not on tablets of stone but on tablets of human hearts" (2 Corinthians 3:2-3). We get to know ourselves through the Holy Spirit.

In our Creed during Mass we confess our faith in the Holy Spirit with these words: "I believe in the Holy Spirit, the Lord, the giver of life." When we make the sign of the cross, as we begin our prayers, we say, "In the name of the Father and of the Son and of the Holy Spirit." And when we conclude our prayers we often say, "Glory be to the Father and to the Son and to the Holy Spirit." But sometimes we can forget to reflect on the role that the Holy Spirit plays in our life and indeed in the future of the world.

Deep down in our hearts we know that we cannot merit the love of God. Sin then begins to whisper in our inner ear that, because we are sinners, incapable of deserving love, God could never love us. And, since we cannot merit God's love, we can never be close to God and we can never really be precious in his sight. St Bernard of Clairvaux, an influential Cistercian monk in the Middle Ages, responded to this false thinking with these powerful words:

> For my part, what I lack of myself, I confidently take to myself from the compassionate heart of the Lord which flows with mercy and which is provided with outlets through which mercy flows… The mercy of the Lord is, then, my merit. I am never bereft of merit as long as he is not bereft of mercy. For if the mercies of the Lord are many, then many are my merits. But what if I am aware of my many sins? Then where sin increased, grace abounded all the more. And if the steadfast love of the Lord is from everlasting to everlasting, then I will sing of the steadfast love of the Lord for ever. And what of my own righteousness? Lord, I shall be mindful only of your righteousness. For your righteousness is also mine since you have been made my righteousness by God.[9]

We have infinite merit because the mercy of God is our merit. This means that God loves us infinitely, not because we are holy but because he wants to share his own holiness with us. By giving us the gift of the Holy Spirit who dwells in our heart, God our Father has prepared us to live a holy life, a life of compassion and love.

Without the Holy Spirit, God the Father's great plan for his human family, in sending Christ to redeem us, will not be realised. Our hearts would remain closed to God. It is only when "the Spirit makes his home" in us that we become spiritually alive, full of thanksgiving to God for his great love, and grateful to Christ for redeeming us and sending us

---

9 Office of Readings, Wednesday, Week 3.

the Spirit through whom we have been "reborn" and become a "new creation" (2 Corinthians 5:17). As St Paul says to us, "Do you not know that you are God's temple and that God's Spirit dwells in you?" (1 Corinthians 3:16).

The gifts of the Spirit

Just before he ascended to heaven after his resurrection from the grave, Jesus made this great promise to his disciples: "You will receive power when the Holy Spirit has come upon you; and you will be my witnesses" (Acts 1:8). This power of the Spirit becomes operational in us through the gifts of the Spirit that we receive at our baptism and confirmation. We often call these special gifts the "charisms" of the Holy Spirit. The Second Vatican Council gave us this clear teaching on the gifts of the Spirit:

> It is not only through the sacraments and the ministries of the Church that the Holy Spirit sanctifies and leads the people of God and enriches it with virtues, but, allotting his gifts to everyone according as He wills, He distributes special graces among the faithful of every rank.[10]

Each baptised person has received special gifts of the Holy Spirit for his or her life and mission in the world. As St John Paul II said:

> The powers of the Spirit, the gifts of the Spirit, and the fruits of the Holy Spirit are revealed in men and women.[11]

It is through these gifts of the Spirit that we receive the power to become witnesses to Christ. Pope Benedict XVI described what it means to become a witness in this way:

> We become witnesses when, through our actions, words and way of being, Another makes himself present.[12]

---

10 Second Vatican Council, *Constitution on the Church*, 12.
11 Pope St John Paul II, *Redemptor Hominis*, 18.
12 Pope Benedict XVI, *Sacramentum Caritatis* ("The Sacrament of Charity"), 85.

We are never alone; we live and work in the Holy Spirit. "Another", that is, Jesus, makes himself present. When a person knows that he/she is going out in Jesus' name, the Holy Spirit is calling that man or woman into a new relationship. Jesus becomes present when the person begins to evangelise and the Holy Spirit will call the person being evangelised to faith in Christ. This is an invisible presence for us, but for those we are trying to help it can seem quite tangible. We don't have to be a great saint before the Holy Spirit can use us in this way. Whenever we are trying to help others in faith, Christ is always present. It is through the Holy Spirit that we are able to share our faith with others. Pope St Paul VI said:

> Evangelization will never be possible without the action of the Holy Spirit... The Holy Spirit places on our lips the words which we could not find by ourselves, and at the same time the Holy Spirit predisposes the soul of the hearer to be open and receptive to the Good News and to the Kingdom being proclaimed.[13]

It is the Holy Spirit who will give you and members of your parish the confidence to become involved in the new evangelisation. We have to be aware that doubts linger. We can begin to ask ourselves, "Am I qualified? Is my parish qualified?" Pope Francis addressed this doubt head on when he stated:

> All the baptized, whatever their position in the Church or their level of instruction in the faith, are agents of evangelization, and it would be insufficient to envisage a plan of evangelization carried out by professionals while the rest of the faithful would remain simply passive.[14]

Each of us has received the gift of the Holy Spirit. We are qualified by the Spirit to share our faith with others, to be witnesses to Christ who has redeemed us. Christ our Lord came into the world to save each person. He wants each person, no matter what their difficulties and no matter how

---

13 Pope St Paul VI, *Evangelization in the Modern World*, 75.
14 Pope Francis, *Evangelii Gaudium* ("The Joy of the Gospel"), 119.

deaf they may seem to be to the promptings of the Spirit in their life, to receive the gift of faith and the blessing of God our Father. The Holy Spirit wants us to share this good news by the way we live and seek to help others. When you find yourself helping someone in need – giving a little money, for instance, to a poor person on the street who is asking for help, or listening to the pain in someone's life – it is the Holy Spirit in you who is inspiring you to do this good work. You have become a witness to Christ. You have brought Christ to the brother or sister whom you have listened to or helped. You may never know the good your generous act has done, but the Holy Spirit will use it for the benefit of the other person whom you have accepted as a brother or sister in Christ in need of help of some kind. The good work that we do for others we do through the power of the Holy Spirit. The more we acknowledge to ourselves the promptings of the Spirit in the good we try to do for others, the more we become aware of the fruits of the Spirit in our life. St Paul tells us that the fruits of the Spirit are "love, joy, peace, patience, kindness, generosity, faithfulness, gentleness, and self-control" (Galatians 5:22-23).

Personal spiritual exercise for internalising the message of this chapter

- Centre yourself; sitting upright; breathing rhythmically; clearing your mind of all preoccupations.
- Bring yourself to bodily stillness.
- Now thank the Lord for the presence of the Holy Spirit in your heart.
- Be still for some time in the presence of God the Father, the Son and the Holy Spirit.
- Now focus again on your breathing as you relax in God's presence.
- And bring yourself gently back to the world.

This spiritual exercise will deepen your awareness of being in the presence of the God of mercy.

CHAPTER FIVE

BAPTISM: BORN AGAIN OF WATER AND THE HOLY SPIRIT

When we accept Christ's invitation to make our home in him, we know we have entered the holiness of God and we feel it necessary to have our minds and hearts purified. That is a sacramentally inspired feeling. Christ has already prepared the way by giving us the holy Sacraments of the Church. The sacrament of baptism is the first and the most important sacrament. As the *Catechism of the Catholic Church* says:

> Holy Baptism is the basis of the whole Christian life, the gateway to life in the Spirit, and the door which gives access to the other sacraments. Through Baptism we are freed from sin and reborn as sons and daughters of God; we become members of Christ, and are incorporated into the Church and made sharers in her mission.[1]

Jesus, when he was speaking to Nicodemus, a leading Pharisee, referred to baptism as "being born of water and Spirit". We will listen in full to this conversation between the Pharisee and Jesus in John's Gospel:

> Now there was a Pharisee named Nicodemus, a leader of the Jews. He came to Jesus by night and said to him, "Rabbi, we know that you are a teacher who has come from God; for no one can do these signs that you do apart from the presence of God." Jesus answered him "Very truly, I tell you, no one can see the kingdom of God without being born from above." Nicodemus said to him "How can anyone be born after having grown old? Can one enter a second time into the mother's womb and be born?" Jesus answered, "Very truly, I tell you, no one can enter the kingdom of God without being born of water and Spirit. What is born of the flesh is flesh, and what is

---

1 *Catechism of the Catholic Church*, Sacrament of Baptism, 1213.

born of the Spirit is spirit. Do not be astonished that I said to you, 'You must be born from above.' The wind blows where it chooses, and you hear the sound of it, but you do not know where it comes from or where it goes. So it is with everyone who is born of the Spirit." Nicodemus said to him, "How can these things be?" Jesus answered him, "Are you a teacher of Israel, and yet you do not understand these things?"

John 3:1-10

Nicodemus went to see Jesus at night because he didn't want his Pharisee colleagues seeing him visiting this upstart teacher. Later on, we find Nicodemus trying to protect Jesus from being arrested. The Pharisees had sent the Temple police to arrest Jesus but they came back without him. They said, "Never has anyone spoken like this." Nicodemus saw his opportunity and asked, "Our law does not judge people without first giving them a hearing to find out what they are doing, does it?" (John 7:51). His fellow Pharisees scorned him. But it was only after the crucifixion that Nicodemus went public as a follower of Jesus. John's Gospel tells us:

> Joseph of Arimathea, who was a disciple of Jesus, though a secret one because of his fear of the Jews, asked Pilate to let him take away the body of Jesus. Pilate gave him permission; so he came and removed his body. Nicodemus, who had at first come to Jesus by night, also came, bringing a mixture of myrrh and aloes, weighing about a hundred pounds. They took the body of Jesus and wrapped it with the spices in linen cloths, according to the burial custom of the Jews.
>
> John 19:38-40

Nicodemus has now gone public about being a follower of Jesus. It is good for us to remember Nicodemus with gratitude, because it was in answer to his questions that the Lord spoke of baptism as being "born of water and Spirit". Each of us now can say, "I have been reborn of water and the Holy Spirit."

Our baptism opened the door for us to the other sacraments. At our baptism, all sin was forgiven. For infants, of course, there were no personal sins that needed forgiveness, but there was still the Original Sin of our first parents, Adam and Eve. They were created by God in a state of holiness and yet when they were tempted by the devil, they disobeyed God. They ate the forbidden fruit. Sin had entered the world. They were expelled by God from the Garden of Eden.

I am sure you have often been amazed to read how the greatest saints see themselves as the greatest sinners. The apostle Paul is a good example. Writing to his collaborator Timothy, he said, "The saying is sure and worthy of full acceptance, that Christ Jesus came into the world to save sinners – of whom I am the foremost. But for that very reason I received mercy, so that in me, as the foremost, Jesus Christ might display the utmost patience, making me an example to those who would come to believe in him for eternal life" (1 Timothy 1:15-17). Paul, or Saul as he was known before his encounter with Jesus Christ, was on his way to Damascus to bring the followers of Jesus back to Jerusalem for condemnation by the high priest of the Temple. St Luke writes:

> Now as he was going along and approaching Damascus, suddenly a light from heaven flashed around him. He fell to the ground and heard a voice saying to him, "Saul, Saul, why do you persecute me?" He asked, "Who are you, Lord?" The reply came, "I am Jesus, whom you are persecuting. But get up and enter the city and you will be told what you are to do."... Saul got up from the ground, and though his eyes were open, he could see nothing; so they led him by the hand and brought him into Damascus. For three days he was without sight, and neither ate nor drank.
>
> Acts 9:3-9

But relief was on the way. The Lord told a disciple by the name of Ananias to go to the house where Saul was and pray over him. So, after a discussion with the Lord, Ananias went to meet Saul. We read, "He laid his hands on Saul and said, 'Brother Saul, the Lord Jesus, who appeared to you on your way here, has sent me so that you may regain your sight and be filled with the Holy Spirit.' And immediately something like scales fell from his eyes, and his sight was restored. Then he got up and was baptized, and after taking some food, he regained his strength" (Acts 9:17-19). Saul had become a Christian. He became the greatest of all the missionary apostles. He proclaimed the Gospel in various parts of Europe and Asia Minor, establishing Christian communities in many places, and was eventually martyred by beheading in Rome about the year AD 68.

Paul is the greatest witness to the truth that Jesus Christ came into the world to save sinners. The devil wants us to believe that poor sinners have no chance of seeing God, because their sins will block them. The opposite, of course, is the truth – every sinner who appeals to Jesus, like the "good" thief on the cross, is welcomed immediately. Jesus recognises each human being as his sister or brother. His love is so abundant that he invites each one of us to make our home in him. He died for the salvation of every human being. Once we commit our lives to the Lord, once we believe with our heart that he is with us for our salvation, we can relax spiritually and open our heart to receive the gifts that the Holy Spirit offers us. We realise the truth of Jesus' promise: "Those who love me will keep my word, and my Father will love them, and we will come to them and make our home with them" (John 14:23).

Our new birth in our baptism

We recall the great sacrament of our baptism. Children of Catholic families are baptised as infants and so they have no memory of receiving that wonderful, life-changing sacrament. It is an outward symbol of the fulfilment of Jesus' declaration that "no one can enter the kingdom of God without being born of water and Spirit" (John 3:5). When parents bring their child to church for baptism, they are proclaiming their faith that their child, through that baptism, will be reborn of water and the Holy Spirit. Our baptism marks our new birth in the Spirit. Our physical birth comes through our mother; our spiritual birth comes through the Holy Spirit. That new birth, in the words of St Peter, gives us a living hope. In his first letter he says, "Blessed be the God and Father of our Lord Jesus Christ! By his great mercy he has given us a new birth into a living hope through the resurrection of Jesus Christ from the dead" (1 Peter 1:3). It is through the Holy Spirit, "the Lord, the giver of life", that our hope remains "a living hope". Without the Holy Spirit we would have no living hope. At our baptism the Holy Spirit gives us a new life, eternal life. Without the Holy Spirit our hope would be a dead hope. We would begin to lose our enthusiasm for life and we would lose the joy that Pope Francis wrote about when he said, "The joy of the Gospel fills the hearts and lives of all who encounter Jesus. Those who accept his offer of salvation are set free from sin, sorrow, inner emptiness and loneliness."[2]

Our living hope

Through our baptism, our first encounter with Jesus, we receive living hope, the spiritual energy that fortifies us and enables us to accept the trials and challenges of each day, by prayerfully offering them to God. We have wonderful prayers such as Psalm 31:5: "Into your hand I commit my spirit; you have redeemed me, O Lord, faithful God." Jesus used this prayer on the cross just before he died (see Luke 23:46). And, of course, Jesus said it with living hope. He knew that the Father's will was being fulfilled. We can have no greater assurance in our life than prayerfully accepting God our Father's will for us each day. During his agony in the garden of Gethsemane, Jesus prayed, "My Father, if it is

---

2 Pope Francis, *Evangelii Gaudium* ("The Joy of the Gospel"), 1.

possible, let this cup pass from me; yet not what I want but what you want" (Matthew 26:39). To joyfully accept God's will for today, we need to live in the grace of our baptism. We gratefully remind ourselves that we have been "born of water and the Holy Spirit"; we need to cultivate the gift of living hope, not just for the bright and good days, but also for the dark and bad days; we need to rejoice in the living hope that enables us to face the future with confidence because we are not facing it alone. The power of the Risen Christ is in us and with us, and we are in him because, at his invitation, we have made our home in him.

Living by the word of God

Jesus tells us that we are to live on "every word that comes from the mouth of God" (Matthew 4:4). Consider the liberating power of this word that God speaks to poor sinners through his prophet:

> Come now, let us talk this over, says the Lord. Though your sins are like scarlet, they become as white as snow; though they are red as crimson, they shall be like wool.
>
> Isaiah 1:18, NJB

This transformation of our sins into holiness when we talk over our life with God reveals to us who our God truly is. As the psalm says, "The Lord is compassion and love, slow to anger and rich in mercy" (Responsorial Psalm 102). God wants each one of us to be embraced by mercy. Pope Francis, when he called the Year of Mercy in 2015, wrote:

> The time has come for the Church to take up the joyful call to mercy once more. It is time to return to the basics and bear the weakness and struggles of our brothers and sisters. Mercy is the force that reawakens us to new life, instils in us the courage to look to the future with hope.[3]

---

3   Pope Francis, *Misericordiae Vultus* ("The Face of Mercy"): Bull of Indiction of the Extraordinary Jubilee Year of Mercy, 2015.

It is with living hope in our hearts that we await the coming of Jesus Christ in glory. St Peter says, "Always have an answer ready for people who ask you the reason for the hope that you have" (1 Peter 3:15, my paraphrase). Our living hope enables us to face the future with peace and trust in our heart. We can calmly face our own death because we believe in eternal life and the resurrection of our body. It is this gift of faith that enables us to serenely surrender our life into God's hands. Prayer is the lifeline that keeps this hope alive and fresh in our heart and keeps us spiritually content as we make our home in Christ.

Baptism opens the door to the full sacramental life of the Church. We are reborn as children of God in the sacrament of baptism. We are now qualified by the Spirit to be witnesses to Christ and to God's plan for the human race. We can share our faith in God with those who ask us. Our faith gives us the reason for the hope that is in us. The Second Vatican Council stated:

> One is right in thinking that the future of humanity rests with people who are capable of providing the generations to come with reasons for living and reasons for hoping.[4]

Who has better reasons for hoping than those who believe that Christ will come again in glory? Who has better reasons for living than those who believe that life in this world is our preparation for our eternal life with God in heaven? Before we can give people reasons for living and hoping, we have to keep that hope alive in our own hearts. We are God's children who have been baptised in the Holy Spirit, whose sins are forgiven each time we turn to Christ our Lord and ask for his forgiveness. Jesus invites us to make our home in him and live not "by bread alone, but by every word that comes from the mouth of God" (Matthew 4:4).

---

4 *Gaudium et Spes* ("The Constitution on the Church in the Modern World"), **31.**

Sharing our faith

It is the Holy Spirit who gives us the confidence to become involved in the new evangelisation; to share our faith with others; to become actively involved in our parish community. But often a doubt lingers. Am I qualified? Is my parish qualified? As we have seen, Pope Francis addressed this doubt head on when he stated:

> All the baptized, whatever their position in the Church or their level of instruction in the faith, are agents of evangelization, and it would be insufficient to envisage a plan of evangelization carried out by professionals while the rest of the faithful would remain simply passive.[5]

At our baptism each of us received the gifts of the Holy Spirit. We are qualified by the Holy Spirit to share our faith with others. We don't need a degree in theology to do that. We share the peace and the joy that baptism enkindled in our heart. As the conversation develops, the Lord will enlighten us. The Holy Spirit will give us the gifts that we need to do this work of sharing our faith with others. The seven gifts of the Holy Spirit that we received in baptism are as follows: "Wisdom, Understanding, Counsel, Fortitude, Knowledge, Piety, and Fear of the Lord. They belong in their fullness to Christ. They complete and perfect the virtues of those who receive them. They make the faithful docile in readily obeying divine inspirations."[6] At your baptism you received these gifts of the Holy Spirit. If you have never had the opportunity to reflect on them or experience them at work in your heart, ask the Holy Spirit now to teach you all about them.

The Holy Spirit also wants us to share the good news of Christ's redemption by the way we live and seek to help others. When you find yourself helping someone in need, giving a little money, for instance, to a poor person on the street who is asking for help, it is the Holy Spirit in you

---
5 Pope Francis, *Evangelii Gaudium*, 119.
6 *Catechism of the Catholic Church*, 1831.

who is inspiring you to do this good work. You have become a witness to Christ and your very act of generosity brings Christ to that brother or sister. You may never know the outcome of your generous act, but the Holy Spirit will use it for the good of the person whom you have accepted as a brother or sister in Christ in need of help of some kind. When we do a good work for others it is most beneficial to remind ourselves that we did it through the inspiration and grace of the Holy Spirit. The more we acknowledge to ourselves the promptings of the Spirit in the good we try to do for others, the more we become aware of the fruits of the Spirit in our lives. St Paul tells us that the fruits of the Spirit are: "love, joy, peace, patience, kindness, goodness, trustfulness, gentleness and self-control" (Galatians 5:22-23, NJB). It can be enlightening to reflect on the fruits of the Spirit, to ask yourself which of them were operational in your responses to others. The first three fruits, "love, joy and peace", are most desirable. Of course, where there is no love there can be no joy or peace either. Indeed, without love none of the other fruits can ripen. They all need to experience love before they can become operational. All the fruits that St Paul mentions require a loving heart.

When we follow the inspiration of the Holy Spirit, we discover that there are many ways in which we can show love and support to the people we work with or to those whom the Lord sends to us to obtain the help they need. We are now recognising the fruits of the Spirit in our lives. When Jesus says in John 15 that we, like branches cut off from the vine, cannot bear fruit unless we remain in him, he is making it clear that whatever good we do, we do it *because* we are abiding in him. We are living by the grace of our baptism. The Holy Spirit is inspiring and guiding us.

These baptismal gifts and fruits that the Lord lavishes on us, when we abide in him, make it possible for us to reach out to our brothers and sisters who need help. Every decision we make and every action we take to offer help and support to someone in need will produce for us a fresh infilling with the Holy Spirit. The words of Jesus will echo in our hearts. He will say to us, "Truly I tell you, just as you did it to one of the least of these who are members of my family, you did it to me" (Matthew 25:40). Now you know that the grace of your baptism is at work in your life. As the *Catechism* teaches:

> By virtue of our Baptism, the first sacrament of the faith, the Holy Spirit in the Church communicates to us, intimately and personally, the life that originates in the Father and is offered to us in the Son.[7]

Our baptism

Children who are baptised as infants are unlikely to have any memories of the occasion. How did it take place? Where did it take place? Who participated in it? What was the structure of the baptismal ceremony? In the Catholic Church, the ministry of the baptism takes place in four different areas of the church: at the door; at the ambo or lectern; at the font; and at the altar. Let us remind ourselves of how this happens.

The door of the church

The family and friends arrive at the church with the baby who is to be baptised. They are met at the door by the priest, who welcomes them. He asks the parents what name they are calling their child. It is recommended that one of the names should be that of a saint, for example Teresa or some other female saint for a girl; John or another male saint for a boy. One of the godparents should be a practising Catholic. The priest then invites the parents and friends to walk up the aisle of the church to the front.

---

[7] *The Catechism of the Catholic Church*, 683.

At the ambo

We now have the proclamation of the word of God from the ambo or lectern. This is followed by a short homily addressed to the parents and friends. The Holy Spirit is in the proclamation of the word. And the Holy Spirit will enter the baby as he or she is baptised. The baby is then anointed with the oil of the catechumens. The priest then places his hands on the baby and prays for God's blessing to descend and remain with him or her.

The font

The water for the baptism is blessed. The priest then asks the parents and godparents two questions:

1. Do you reject Satan and all his works and all his empty promises?

   Response: I do.

2. Do you believe in God the Father almighty, Creator of heaven and earth?

   Response: I do.

The baptism now takes place. The priest pours water over the head of the child and says, "I baptise you in the name of the Father and of the Son and of the Holy Spirit." The Holy Spirit comes down at this moment and remains with the baby, who is now a child of God.

The baby is now anointed with the oil of chrism. A candle is lit from the Paschal Candle and the priest hands it to the parents, saying, "Receive the light of Christ. May he/she keep the flame of Christ alive in his/her heart."

The altar

The baptismal ceremony is concluded at the altar. The priest leads the family in saying the Lord's Prayer together. He then blesses the mother, the father and finally the godparents.

The great sacrament of baptism has been celebrated and the child has now become a member of Christ's body. As St Paul says, "For just as the body is one and has many members, and all the members of the body, though many, are one body, so it is with Christ. For in the one Spirit we were all baptized into one body – Jews or Greeks, slaves or free – and we were all made to drink of one Spirit" (1 Corinthians 12:12-13).

The child's Christian life has now begun. How it will develop and grow depends largely on how its parents and godparents live their own Christian lives. If they are people of prayer, who pray together, they will invite their growing child to join them in prayer. The child will then learn how to pray. More significantly, as the child begins to mature as a young boy or girl, prayer time will be recognised as a significant moment in the daily life of the family. When the young man or woman leaves home, this memory of the family prayer time will stay with them. They will have learned a great deal about prayer and will be well prepared to continue their life of prayer alone.

Our prayer time

Prayer is our lifeline from and to God. God has given us this gift, and because it is such a lifeline it should always be accorded priority time. We have many fixed times for doing our various daily tasks: time for getting up and going to bed; time for getting the kids to school and, if possible, being at home when they come back; time for breakfast, lunch and evening meal; time for going to work and coming back from work; time when the family needs our full attention; time for relaxation, for watching TV, reading a book or listening to music or the radio. And somewhere in this busy timetable we have time to pray. That should be a priority.

Where do you schedule your prayer time? What priority does it have in your daily timetable? Experience teaches most people that if prayer is not the top priority in their day, it will take second place to every other good work that has to be done. If my prayer time is not my top priority then I may find myself saying, "I will pray when I have the time" or "I will pray when I feel like it." If I plan my prayer life along those lines, I will quickly discover that I have less and less time and less and less inclination. If I am not breathing in sufficient spiritual oxygen through my lifeline of prayer, I will begin to suffer from spiritual under-nourishment. I cannot live a spiritual life without the basic spiritual nourishment that prayer provides. St Alphonsus Liguori put it this way:

> As moisture is necessary for the life of plants to prevent them from drying up, so, says St. Chrysostom, is prayer necessary for our salvation. Prayer vivifies the soul, as the soul vivifies the body. Prayer is also called the food of the soul, because the body cannot be supported without food; nor can the soul, says St. Augustine, be kept alive without prayer: "As flesh is nourished by food, so is man supported by prayers." All these comparisons used by the holy Fathers are intended by them to teach the absolute necessity of prayer for the salvation of everyone.[8]

Because prayer is so important for our spiritual well-being, Jesus encourages us to make it a priority in our daily schedule with these words:

> So I say to you, Ask, and it will be given to you; search, and you will find; knock, and the door will be opened for you. For everyone who asks receives, and everyone who searches finds, and for everyone who knocks, the door will be opened.

---

8 St Alphonsus Liguori, *Prayer: The Great Means of Salvation and of Perfection* (Edmond, OK: Veritatis Splendor Publications, 2012, edited by Paul A. Boer, Sr), 10.

> Is there anyone among you who, if your child asks for a fish, will give a snake instead of a fish? Or if the child asks for an egg, will give a scorpion? If you then, who are evil, know how to give good gifts to your children, how much more will the heavenly Father give the Holy Spirit to those who ask him!
>
> Luke 11:9-13

The Holy Spirit is the gift that God the Father gave to us on the day of our baptism. Since then, the Holy Spirit has made a home in our heart and encourages us to accept the invitation that Jesus makes to each of us when he says, "Make your home in me as I make mine in you." Let us accept this invitation each day. We receive this grace and the presence of the Spirit when we humbly ask God to pour out his Spirit in our life. St Paul sums up the life of the baptised in this way:

> So if you have been raised with Christ, seek the things that are above, where Christ is, seated at the right hand of God. Set your minds on things that are above, not on things that are on earth, for you have died, and your life is hidden with Christ in God. When Christ who is your life is revealed, then you also will be revealed with him in glory.
>
> Colossians 3:1-4

The *Catechism of the Catholic Church* clarifies the implications of this for us in this way:

> This outpouring of mercy cannot penetrate our hearts as long as we have not forgiven those who have trespassed against us. Love, like the Body of Christ, is indivisible; we cannot love the God we cannot see if we do not love the brother or sister we do see. In refusing to forgive our brothers or sisters, our hearts are closed and their hardness makes them impervious to the Father's merciful love; but in confessing our sins, our hearts are opened to his grace.[9]

---

9 *Catechism of the Catholic Church*, 2840.

As baptised adults, we know the mystery of our baptism, the mystery of being washed clean in our human spirit by the infilling with God's Holy Spirit. Each new day we welcome the Spirit of God afresh into our heart and with the Spirit's divine power we commit ourselves to living the new life in the Spirit that God has given to us.

> **Personal spiritual exercise for internalising the message of this chapter**
>
> - Centre yourself; sitting upright; breathing rhythmically; clearing your mind of all preoccupations.
> - Bring yourself to bodily stillness.
> - Now renew your faith and say to yourself, "My baptism was my new birth in the Holy Spirit." As you ponder your new birth, ask the Holy Spirit to enlighten you.
> - Be still for some time in the presence of the God of mercy and compassion and receive his love.
> - Now focus again on your breathing as you relax in God's presence.
> - And bring yourself gently back to the world.

This spiritual exercise will deepen your awareness of being in the presence of the God of grace and show you how God has embraced you with his love and mercy.

CHAPTER SIX

MAKING OUR HOME IN CHRIST THROUGH THE EUCHARIST

At the heart of our Christian faith is the belief that Jesus, while he was sharing the Passover Meal, his last supper with his apostles, took bread, blessed it and said, "Take, eat; this is my body." Then he took a cup, and after giving thanks he gave it to them, saying, "Drink from it, all of you; for this is my blood of the covenant, which is poured out for many for the forgiveness of sins" (Matthew 26:26-28). Knowing that he would be condemned to die on a cross the next day, Good Friday, Jesus gave himself to his apostles and to all who would believe in him down through the centuries, under the appearance of bread and wine. As the *Catechism of the Catholic Church* says, "The Eucharist is the sum and the summary of our faith; our way of thinking is attuned to the Eucharist, and the Eucharist confirms our way of thinking."[1]

Jesus, who invites us to make our home in him, gave us this golden opportunity to do that when he initiated the holy Eucharist at the Last Supper. Our way of living, of acting, of relating to others is also attuned to the Eucharist. Through celebrating the Eucharist, our life becomes eucharistic. This is how Jesus responded to those who rejected his gift of himself in the Eucharist:

> Very truly, I tell you, unless you eat the flesh of the Son of Man and drink his blood, you have no life in you. Those who eat my flesh and drink my blood have eternal life, and I will raise them up on the last day; for my flesh is true food and my blood is true drink. Those who eat my flesh and drink my blood abide in me, and I in them. Just as the living Father sent me, and I live because of the Father, so whoever eats me will live because of me.
>
> John 6:53-57

---

1 *Catechism of the Catholic Church*, 1327.

Today we can gratefully say that we are a eucharistic people abiding in Christ, making our home in Christ, because we share in the body and blood of Jesus, our Saviour.

Our gathering together to celebrate the Mass manifests the unity of the Church. Indeed, it is through our celebration of the Mass that we express in our lives the whole mystery of Christ. The Second Vatican Council reminded us:

> The liturgy, through which "the work of our redemption takes place", especially in the divine sacrifice of the Eucharist, is supremely effective in enabling the faithful to express in their lives and portray to others the mystery of Christ and the real nature of the Church.[2]

We are not just worshipping God by going to Mass, we are also manifesting to ourselves and to others the "real nature of the Church". As the great Orthodox theologian Alexander Schmemann wrote:

> The Eucharist is not "one of the sacraments" or one of the services, but the very manifestation and fulfillment of the Church in all her power, sanctity and fullness.[3]

The official *Catechism of the Catholic Church* agrees with what Schmemann wrote. It reminds us that:

> The Eucharist is the "source and summit" of the Christian life. The other sacraments, and indeed all ecclesiastical ministries and works of the apostolate, are bound up with the Eucharist and are oriented to it. For in the blessed Eucharist is contained the whole spiritual good of the Church, namely Christ himself, our Pasch.[4]

As we gather for the Mass, this manifestation of the Church begins to happen. Christ is present in each person who comes to Mass. We have to open our eye of faith to recognise his presence in each brother and sister with whom we are

---

[2] Second Vatican Council, *Constitution on the Sacred Liturgy*, 2.
[3] Alexander Schmemann, *The Eucharist* (New York: St Vladimir's Seminary Press, 1997), 25.
[4] *Catechism of the Catholic Church*, 1324.

celebrating the Mass. Christ is as truly present in a small congregation of a few dozen as he is within a congregation of thousands. Both congregations, the small and the large, are manifestations of the Church and embody the presence of Christ. A Mass that is celebrated by the small community of ten gives the same glory to God as a Mass celebrated by a community of ten thousand.

As if we had been present there

St John Paul II told us why Jesus chose to leave us the Eucharist:

> When the Church celebrates the Eucharist, the memorial of her Lord's death and resurrection, this central event of salvation becomes really present and "the work of our redemption is carried out". This sacrifice is so decisive for the salvation of the human race that Jesus Christ offered it and returned to the Father only *after he had left us a means of sharing in it* as if we had been present there.[5]

As if we had been present there! We are at no disadvantage that we weren't in that Upper Room with Jesus and the apostles for that Last Supper, the Eucharist, because when we are at Mass we are basically experiencing what the apostles did on that first Holy Thursday evening, the evening before Christ was crucified, the evening when Jesus gave his body and blood for our salvation. Evil will not gain the final victory. Christ, in dying for us and in giving us the Eucharist, has delivered humanity from ultimate evil. The Eucharist is the supreme act of the love of Jesus for each one of us. Each of us can say to Jesus, "You died for me." With our whole being we seek to participate contemplatively in the celebration of the Mass. As we begin, the priest greets us with these words: "The grace of our Lord Jesus Christ, and the love of God, and the communion of the Holy Spirit be with you all." The priest then says, "Brothers and

---

5 St John Paul II, *Ecclesia de Eucharistia*, 11.

sisters, let us acknowledge our sins and so prepare ourselves to celebrate the sacred mysteries." Now we know where we are: we are in God's presence, and we are asking for his forgiveness as the priest prays, "May almighty God have mercy on us, forgive us our sins, and bring us to everlasting life." We now thank the Lord for his mercy and compassion by saying the beautiful prayer of praise that we call the Gloria. Let us remind ourselves once again of the beauty of this prayer:

> Glory to God in the highest,
> and on earth peace to people of good will.
> We praise you, we bless you,
> we adore you, we glorify you,
> we give you thanks for your great glory,
> Lord God, heavenly King,
> O God, almighty Father.
> Lord Jesus Christ,
> Only Begotten Son,
> Lord God, Lamb of God,
> Son of the Father,
> you take away the sins of the world,
> have mercy on us;
> you take away the sins of the world,
> receive our prayer;
> you are seated at the right hand of the Father,
> have mercy on us.
> For you alone are the Holy One,
> you alone are the Lord,
> you alone are the Most High, Jesus Christ,
> with the Holy Spirit,
> in the glory of God the Father. Amen.

Having said this beautiful Gloria prayer at our Sunday Mass, we are now ready to settle down and listen to God's word. We are engaged in four different activities at each service: we listen, we respond, we offer and we receive. We will reflect on these four prayerful responses that are made as we celebrate the Holy Eucharist at Mass.

We listen

God speaks to us through readings from the Old Testament, from the Epistles in the New Testament and from one of the four Gospels written by Matthew, Mark, Luke and John. Because it is God who is speaking to us, we do our best to listen. This stage of the Mass is called the *Liturgy of the Word*. We know from experience that sometimes we can find it hard to listen. Distractions can be the biggest obstacles we have to overcome as we listen to God's word. Our thoughts can be all over the place. When we become aware that our thoughts are elsewhere as the scripture is being proclaimed, we can gently say a prayer such as, "Come, Holy Spirit, give me the grace to listen to God's word with my whole heart." Then we start again to listen calmly. We believe that the life-giving word of God has the answers to all our problems. Pope Benedict XVI reminded us:

> It is decisive, from the pastoral standpoint, to present the word of God in its capacity to enter into dialogue with the everyday problems which people face... We need to make every effort to share the word of God as an openness to our problems, a response to our questions, a broadening of our values and the fulfilment of our aspirations.[6]

God wants to be in dialogue with you about everything that is going on in your life. The Holy Spirit enlightens your mind and enables you, even in very dark or threatening moments, to find the presence of God. The Holy Spirit reminds you that Christ invites you to make your home in him. With the gift of faith in God you are never alone, because you believe God is always with you. You believe that Christ your Saviour has invited you to make your home in him. Even in the darkest moment the light of God shines in your heart. As God said through the great prophet Isaiah, "For I, the Lord your God, hold your right hand; it is I who say to you, 'Do not fear, I will help you'" (Isaiah 41:13). Claim now that promise God has made to you. He will help you by means of the indwelling

---

[6] Pope Benedict XVI, *Verbum Domini*, 23.

presence of the Holy Spirit. Pope Francis said, "When the Holy Spirit dwells in our hearts and enlightens our minds, he makes us grow day by day in the understanding of what the Lord has said and accomplished."[7] Our constant prayer at all times of doubt or worry or fear should be, "Come, Holy Spirit."

Hearing the word of God

As we allow the Holy Spirit to open our hearts, we will begin to receive the words of scripture in a new way. Scripture tells us that "the word of God is living and active" (Hebrews 4:12). It is not a word from the past, about some situation that occurred long ago. God is speaking to us in the present; it is a life-giving gift for today. But without faith we will not be able to accept scripture as God's word. Our interior attitude as we listen to the scriptures being proclaimed should always be "Speak, Lord, for your servant is listening" (1 Samuel 3:9); we hear the word of God with our ears; we receive that word in our mind; but it is the Holy Spirit who enables the divine truth expressed by the words to permeate our heart. If my heart is closed to the word, I may hear it with my ears, but it will not penetrate to the depths of my being. God speaks to us directly through the words of scripture. As the Second Vatican Council said:

> In the sacred books the Father who is in heaven comes lovingly to meet his children and talks with them. And such is the force and the power of the word of God that it is the church's support and strength, imparting robustness to the faith of its daughters and sons and providing food for their souls. It is a pure and unfailing fount to spiritual life.[8]

---

7 Pope Francis, *General Audience*, 30 April 2014.
8 Second Vatican Council, *Dogmatic Constitution on Divine Revelation*, 2111.

Healing faith

St Thomas Aquinas said:

> The letter even of the Gospel would kill were there not the inward grace of healing faith.[9]

Without a healing faith in Christ's presence in the Blessed Sacrament, we cannot receive Holy Communion. Likewise, without a healing faith we will not be able to hear the word of God as the scriptures are being proclaimed. Invoking the Holy Spirit to enlighten our mind as we listen to a sermon or talk is the necessary preparation for receiving the word of God. If we do our best to listen to the word of God being proclaimed at Mass, the Holy Spirit will guide us and prepare us to open our heart to the Lord. In the solemn moments of the Mass, it is always beneficial to remind ourselves that the Holy Spirit dwells within us and will enlighten our mind and our understanding.

We respond

When God speaks to us through his holy word, the whole congregation responds. Our responses should flow from our hearts. The reader leads us with a psalm of thanksgiving and after each verse the congregation responds with thanks to God. Some of those responses are: *I will sing for ever of your love, O Lord*; or, *From all my terrors the Lord sets me free*; or *The Lord is my shepherd; there is nothing I shall want*. These responses open our hearts to welcome the word of God. Jesus says, "Blessed ... are those who hear the word of God and obey it!" (Luke 11:28).

While it is very helpful to have some knowledge of the Bible, we do not need to be experts as we listen to the word of God. We have to remind ourselves that God is coming to speak to us, and ask for the grace to welcome his word.

---

9 *Summa Theologica*,1a-IIae.q. 106, part 2.

The first thing we have to realise each time we hear the scriptures proclaimed at church is that these words are not just the words of some ancient writer, a Jeremiah or a Paul or a Peter, but that God himself, using the words of those ancient writers, is now speaking to us. St Paul, for instance, in writing to the Christian communities in Rome or in Corinth, was teaching them the faith in Christ that they had accepted. But the deeper reality of what Paul had to say was the fact that the Holy Spirit used his words to speak not just to the first-century Christians to whom he was writing, but to the twenty-first-century Christians who hear his words today – to us. Through St Paul's words the Holy Spirit speaks to us each time we hear them proclaimed at Mass or each time we read his letters privately. When the Gospel is being proclaimed, it is Jesus himself who is speaking directly to us.

We offer

We move from listening to the word of God to giving God our gifts. The offertory during the Mass is the time when delegated members of the congregation bring our gifts of bread and wine to the altar and present them to the priest, and the priest then offers them to God. The collection is often taken up at this time and the organist may play a hymn for the congregation to sing.

The offertory is a very significant time in the celebration of the Mass. Sometimes we may overlook its full significance. St Paul, in his letter to the Romans, said, "I appeal to you…, brothers and sisters, by the mercies of God, to present your bodies as a living sacrifice, holy and acceptable to God" (Romans 12:1). Commenting on these words, Pope Benedict XVI said:

> In these words the new worship appears as a total self-offering made in communion with the whole Church. The Apostle's insistence on the offering of our bodies emphasizes the concrete human reality of a worship which is anything but disincarnate.[10]

---

10 Pope Benedict XVI, *Heart of the Christian Life* (San Francisco: Ignatius Press, 2010), 75.

Our self-offering

The bread and wine that we offer to God represent the total self-offering that we are making to God. The only gift we have for God is the gift of ourselves. As we offer ourselves to God, deep inner healing will take place in our hearts. We know that the bread and wine that the priest offers to God represent ourselves and all that is within us. We are offering to God all our joys and sorrows, all our hurts and inner wounds; our disappointments and our frustrations; our family upsets and our struggles with colleagues at work; our grief at the death of a loved one or the pain of a marriage break-up, and every other suffering that we experience. We offer all our inner pains and disappointments to God as the bread and wine are being offered by the priest. This can be a moment of great purification and healing if we surrender our whole being to God. The Lord knows everything and he invites us lovingly and trustingly to offer him everything.

The celebrant, offering our gifts that represent ourselves and all that is within us to God, says on our behalf:

> Blessed are you, Lord God of all creation, for through your goodness we have received the bread we offer you: fruit of the earth and work of human hands, it will become for us the bread of life.

Then the priest pours the wine that we have offered into the chalice and adds a drop of water, silently saying this remarkable prayer: "By the mystery of this water and wine may we come to share in the divinity of Christ, who humbled himself to share in our humanity." In this prayer we are claiming our true identity and our true destiny. Now we are not just offering our gifts to God; we are asking that God give us a share in the very divinity of Jesus, the Son of God. We have to ponder that request deeply. We believe that God is our loving Father and Creator. He made us in his own image and likeness. We should be the visible manifestation of God in our world. But, alas, we have sinned. We need salvation.

And so, in the Mass, we acknowledge our sinfulness before God and open our hearts to receive his mercy and forgiveness. That is why we are bringing our gifts to the altar. And, in the very act of gift-giving, the expression of our love for God, we are emboldened to make that extraordinary request: "May we share in the divinity of Christ." The reason we give for this bold request is: "Christ humbled himself to share in our humanity." This wonderful request is made silently by the priest in our name. He prays, "May we share in the divinity of Christ, who humbled himself to share in our humanity." At every Mass offered throughout the world, that request is made to God. Often the congregation remain totally unaware that the priest is praying for this wonderful divinisation of their lives. We should remind ourselves frequently that the Mass is being offered for our divinisation, for our making our home in Christ. Jesus says to us, "I am the true vine, and my Father is the vine-grower... Abide in me as I abide in you. Just as the branch cannot bear fruit by itself unless it abides in the vine, neither can you unless you abide in me. I am the vine, you are the branches" (John 15:1-5).

Participation

We are participants in the celebration of the Mass, not mere spectators. Our *going* to Mass becomes celebrating the Mass, which is the action of the whole congregation. As *The General Instruction of the Roman Missal* says:

> In the celebration of Mass the faithful form a holy people, a people of God's own possession and a royal Priesthood, so that they may give thanks to God and offer the unblemished sacrificial Victim not only by means of the hands of the Priest but also together with him and so that they may learn to offer their very selves.[11]

---

11 *The General Instruction of the Roman Missal* © 2011, Catholic Bishops' Conference of England and Wales, 95.

In those two fundamental offerings that we all make at Mass, we offer "the unblemished sacrificial victim", that is Jesus, with the priest, and we learn to offer ourselves to God.

We assemble for Mass to make that twofold offering, not as isolated individuals but as members of the one body of Christ, the community of the faithful, the Sunday congregation. As the *General Instruction* emphasises:

> [The faithful] are to form one body, whether in hearing the word of God, or by taking part in the prayers and in the singing, or above all by the common offering of the Sacrifice and by participating together at the Lord's table.[12]

The Consecration

Our gifts of bread and wine, representing the gift that we are making of ourselves to God, are now placed on the altar. The priest, acting as the very person of Christ, imposes his hands over our gifts on the altar and says the prayers of consecration:

> Make holy, therefore, these gifts, we pray, by sending down your Spirit upon them like the dewfall, so that they may become for us the Body and Blood of our Lord Jesus Christ. At the time he was betrayed and entered willingly into his Passion, He took bread, and giving thanks, broke it, and gave it to his disciples saying: Take this, all of you, and eat of it, for this is My Body, which will be given for you.

> In a similar way, when supper was ended, he took the chalice and once more giving thanks, he gave it to his disciples, saying: Take this, all of you, and drink from it, for this is the chalice of my Blood, the Blood of the new and eternal Covenant, which will be poured out for you and for many for the forgiveness of sins. Do this in memory of me.

---

12 *General Instruction of the Roman Missal*, 95.

After the elevation of the precious Blood of Christ in the chalice, the priest proclaims **the mystery of faith**. The consecration of the bread and wine into the Body and Blood of Christ is truly the mystery of our faith. Without that faith we would not be able to believe.

When we respond with the acclamation, "We proclaim your death, O Lord, and profess your resurrection, until you come again", we are praying for Christ's coming in glory. In fact, we are saying, "Until you come again we will continue to do what we are doing, namely, proclaiming your death and resurrection in the celebration of the Mass."

We receive

The gifts of bread and wine that we offered to God have now, through the power of the Holy Spirit, become the Body and Blood of Christ. Jesus Christ is now truly present on the altar. It is the gift of faith that enables us to believe this mystery of God's love and tenderness. Without faith we could never believe in the mystery of the Mass. Christ, our brother and Redeemer, who died for our sins, is now present on the altar waiting for us to come forward and receive him in Holy Communion. After the consecration the community prays:

> Look, we pray, upon the oblation of your Church and recognizing the sacrificial Victim by whose death you willed to reconcile us to yourself, grant that we, who are nourished by the Body and Blood of your Son and filled with his Holy Spirit, may become one body, one spirit in Christ (Third Eucharistic Prayer).

> Humbly we pray that, partaking of the Body and Blood of Christ, we may be gathered into one by the Holy Spirit (Second Eucharistic Prayer).

These prayers are the profound request that the eucharistic community makes to God our Father. Pope Francis encourages us, "Let us always remember that it is the Church, the Body of Christ, that is the celebrating subject and not just the priest." When you participate in Mass you are united in the celebration with every other participant. That is why we pray that we may "be gathered into one by the Holy Spirit". Pope Benedict XVI explained this well when he wrote:

> The Eucharist is the sacrament of communion between brothers and sisters who allow themselves to be reconciled in Christ, who made of Jews and pagans one people, tearing down the wall of hostility which divided them (cf. Ephesians 2:14). Only this constant impulse towards reconciliation enables us to partake worthily of the Body and Blood of Christ.[13]

As we approach the altar to receive Holy Communion, we must have love in our hearts for every person. Jesus says, "When you are offering your gift at the altar, if you remember that your brother or sister has something against you, leave your gift there before the altar and go; first be reconciled to your brother or sister, and then come and offer your gift" (Matthew 5:23-24). When we are opening our hearts to receive Christ in Holy Communion, we have the inner power to forgive and be reconciled. Pope St Leo the Great, who became Pope in AD 440, explained this well when he said, "Our partaking of the Body and Blood of Christ tends only to make us become what we eat."[14] We eat the body of Christ in Holy Communion and we become the body of Christ in the world. And as the body of Christ we have the inner power to forgive from the heart. We begin to love as Christ loves and to forgive as Christ forgives. While he was hanging on the cross in pain Jesus cried out, "Father, forgive them; for they do not know what they are doing" (Luke 23:34). On the superficial level the High Priests and Pharisees knew exactly what they were doing: they were getting rid of the man who was challenging their way of life and leading their followers astray. But at the deeper level of their heart they didn't know that it was God himself who was empowering this man, Jesus from Nazareth, to do what he was doing.

---

13 Pope Benedict XVI, *Sacramentum Caritatis* ("The Sacrament of Charity"), 89.
14 Pope St Leo the Great, *Sermon 12 on the Passion*, in Raniero Cantalamessa, *The Eucharist* (Collegeville, MN: Liturgical Press, 1995), 39.

Jesus was empowered to forgive his persecutors and he empowers us to imitate him and forgive from our hearts all those who hurt or offend us.

Holy Communion

Christ enters our hearts in Holy Communion to so transform us that we become his body in this world. The living bread that we eat in Holy Communion is not transformed into our body; rather, we are transformed into Christ's body. St Augustine expressed this amazing truth in this way:

> If you are the body and members of Christ, then it is your sacrament that is placed on the table of the Lord; it is your sacrament that you receive. To that which you respond, "Amen" ("yes, it is true") and by responding to it you assent to it. For you hear the words, "the Body of Christ" and respond "Amen". Be then a member of the Body of Christ so that your Amen may be true.[15]

Our Holy Communion, therefore, is much more than receiving Christ into our hearts, wonderful though that is. It is Christ receiving us so completely into *his* heart that we become one in spirit with him. Each time we receive Holy Communion, we become more deeply one with Christ.

Sharing Christ's hour

St John introduces his account of the Last Supper and Passion with these words: "Now before the festival of the Passover, Jesus knew that his hour had come to depart from this world and go to the Father" (John 13:1). Jesus wants us to be with him in his hour. As Pope Benedict XVI said:

> Jesus left us the task of entering into his "hour". The Eucharist draws us into Jesus' act of self-oblation. More than just statically receiving the incarnate Word, we enter into the very dynamic of his self-giving.[16]

---
15 St Augustine, cited in *The Catechism of the Catholic Church*, 1396.
16 Pope Benedict XVI, *Sacramentum Caritatis*, 11.

Our response to Christ's self-giving love is our own desire to reciprocate with self-giving love by entering into Holy Communion with Christ. And, no matter how half-hearted we may feel we are, once we "enter into the very dynamic of Christ's self-giving", our own self-giving is purified and enlivened and enables us to discover our true selves. As the Vatican Council said, "We can only discover our true selves in sincere self-giving."[17] In our Holy Communion, Christ shares with us the "dynamic of his self-giving" and activates and strengthens our own self-giving. During our Sunday Mass we receive Christ and we become Christ for the coming week.

The Holy Trinity and Holy Communion

Our union with Jesus in Holy Communion is so personal and intimate that we may often overlook its deeper mystery. When the apostle Philip said to Jesus, "Lord, show us the Father, and we will be satisfied," Jesus said to him, "Have I been with you all this time, Philip, and you still do not know me? Whoever has seen me has seen the Father. How can you say, 'Show us the Father'? Do you not believe that I am in the Father and the Father is in me?" (John 14:8-10). Jesus continued this talk with his disciples by saying, "I will not leave you orphaned; I am coming to you. In a little while the world will no longer see me, but you will see me; because I live, you also will live. On that day you will know that I am in my Father, and you in me, and I in you" (John 14:18-20). Jesus is revealing to us the profound mystery that we are his Father's beloved sons and daughters; we are God's sinful children whom he has redeemed by sending us God the Son who came among us as Jesus the son of Mary and laid down his life for our salvation. Jesus dwells in us today and asks us to make our home in him. Will you accept his invitation?

---

17 Second Vatican Council, *Constitution on the Church in the Modern World*, 34.

Let us listen to the prayer that Jesus says to his Father for each of us:

> I ask not only on behalf of these, but also on behalf of those who will believe in me through their word, that they may all be one. As you, Father, are in me and I am in you, may they also be in us, so that the world may believe that you have sent me. The glory that you have given me I have given them, so that they may be one, as we are one, I in them and you in me, that they may become completely one, so that the world may know that you have sent me and have loved them even as you have loved me.
>
> John 17:20-23

This great prayer that Jesus made to God the Father is fulfilled in our Holy Communion. We enter into communion not only with Jesus but also with the Father, and not just with the Father but also with one another. In the Eucharist the Holy Spirit gives us Christ in the consecration, and Christ gives us the Holy Spirit in the Communion.

Our Communion in Mass manifests the profound mystery of our Church. As the Second Vatican Council said:

> The Church is a people made one with the unity of the Father, the Son and the Holy Spirit.[18]

This unity becomes manifest in the congregation as we move as one body to receive the Body and Blood of Jesus. We are not approaching the altar as isolated individuals. We are coming as "a people made one", as the body of Christ. Our intimate, personal relationship with Jesus in Holy Communion is never an individualistic one. It cannot be reduced to "me and my Jesus". It is always a communitarian relationship, a trinitarian relationship, while being at the same time deeply personal and intimate. In our thanksgiving we should acknowledge that it is from the Father and

---

18 Second Vatican Council, *Constitution on the Church in the Modern World*, 4.

through the Holy Spirit that we have received the gift of Jesus in Holy Communion. If, as Jesus said to Philip, "to see me is to see the Father", then surely it is also true that to receive Jesus is to receive the Father. It is good and at times, perhaps, necessary to remind ourselves that each of us equally receives Jesus and with him the Father and the Holy Spirit in Holy Communion. No one receives more than anyone else. We are God's family.

Personal spiritual exercise for internalising the message of this chapter

- Centre yourself; sitting upright; breathing rhythmically; clearing your mind of all preoccupations.
- Bring yourself to bodily stillness.
- Now gratefully thank the Lord for the gift of himself in the Holy Eucharist and ask him to sanctify and purify your whole being.
- Be still for some time in the presence of the God of mercy and compassion and receive his love.
- Now focus again on your breathing as you relax in God's presence.
- And bring yourself gently back to the world.

This spiritual exercise will deepen your awareness of receiving the Body and Blood of Jesus in Holy Communion.

CHAPTER SEVEN

THE SACRAMENT OF RECONCILIATION AND HEALING

After his resurrection, Jesus appeared to his disciples on Easter Sunday evening and greeted them with the words: "Peace be with you." Then he breathed on them and said, "Receive the Holy Spirit. If you forgive the sins of any, they are forgiven them; if you retain the sins of any, they are retained" (John 20:21-23). At that very moment the disciples received the authority to forgive sins in Jesus' name. That authority is still alive and active in the Church today. We are all poor sinners and we all need to receive forgiveness for our sins. But we have to take the first step by approaching the throne of mercy. As the scripture says, "Let us therefore approach the throne of grace with boldness, so that we may receive mercy and find grace to help in time of need" (Hebrews 4:16). Instead of holding on to our guilt, our wounds and our fears, we are invited by God to come confidently to the throne of grace where Christ, the mercy of the Father, embraces us and makes us feel at home in him. As St Peter assures us, "Once you had not received mercy, but now you have received mercy" (1 Peter 2:10). We can now lay all our sins, our wounds and fears, our anxieties and worries at the feet of Christ who welcomes us as he says, "Make your home in me as I make mine in you" (John 15:4, my paraphrase).

Sin is an offence against God but it also inflicts a wound, not only on the sinner but also on his or her victim and indeed on the whole Church. Parents sin by neglecting their children, but they also wound their children. Nothing inflicts a deeper wound on a child than the sense that he or she is not unconditionally loved and accepted by father or mother. Such children will grow up insecure and lacking in positive self-esteem. Children sin by abandoning their parents and not showing them gratitude and love, but they also wound their parents by such a lack of love. Parents can receive no greater wound than the realisation that their adult sons or daughters have little or no time for them. This wound can cause parents to end their days in bitterness of heart.

We don't have to live with sin. For the sin itself there is forgiveness; for the wound of sin there is healing. The wound of sin is an inner one. The person is wounded in his or her self-esteem, self-image, relationships or memory. In the sacrament of reconciliation there is healing for all these inner wounds.

Catholics are familiar with the sacrament of reconciliation, which we also call the sacrament of confession. Carl Jung, the famous Swiss psychologist and founder of analytical psychology, had a high regard for the Catholic sacrament of confession. He wasn't a Catholic but he observed the effects of religious convictions on all people. Writing about the Catholic practice of confession, he said:

> The fact is there are relatively few neurotic Catholics, and yet they are living under the same conditions as we do. They are presumably suffering from the same social conditions and so on, and so one would expect a similar amount of neurosis. There must be something in the cult, in the actual religious practice, which explains that peculiar fact that there are fewer complexes, or that these complexes manifest themselves much less in Catholic than in other people. That something, besides confession, is really the cult itself. It is the Mass, for instance.[1]

For Jung, confession was the central sacrament in the Catholic tradition that explained why so many Catholics were free from "neurotic manifestations". So he wrote:

> You find the least or smallest number of complex manifestations in practising Catholics, far more in Protestants, and most in Jews... So there must be something in the Catholic Church which accounts for this peculiar fact. Of course, we think in the first place of confession.[2]

---
1 C. G. Jung, *The Collected Works* (London: Routledge & Kegan Paul Ltd, 1977), vol. 18, para. 613.
2 Ibid., vol. 18, para. 612/3.

Sacrament of confession

The sacrament of confession brings the penitent person into the very presence of the God who takes away all his or her sins through the power of the Holy Spirit. As the priest begins to absolve the penitent, he prays:

> God, the Father of mercies, through the death and resurrection of his Son Jesus has reconciled the world to himself and sent the Holy Spirit among us for the forgiveness of sins.

The forgiveness of our sins is the redemptive deed of the Blessed Trinity. God, the Father of mercies, by the death of Jesus, his Son who died on the cross for our salvation, fills the heart of the penitent with the Holy Spirit and the Holy Spirit takes away all our sins. The repentant sinner is completely cleansed in the sanctifying waters of the Spirit as the priest says, in the name of Jesus, "I absolve you from all your sins in the name of the Father and of the Son and of the Holy Spirit." In that very moment it is the "Father of mercies" who welcomes and embraces the repentant penitent. All sins are forgiven and the wounds of sin are healed. But the repentant penitent has to forgive those who inflicted a wound on his or her heart. Just as we ask God to forgive us for our offences, so we promise God to forgive those who offended us.

In the very act of absolving the penitent, the priest emphasises the fact that it is the Holy Spirit, now present with us in Christ's sacrament of reconciliation, who is the forgiveness of sins and who takes away our sins.

The role of the confessor

The rite of the sacrament of reconciliation describes the confessor's role in this way:

> By receiving repentant sinners and leading them to the light of the truth, the confessor fulfils a paternal function: he reveals the heart of the Father and shows the image of Christ the Good Shepherd. He should keep in mind that he has

been entrusted with the ministry of Christ, who mercifully accomplished the saving work of human redemption and by mercy and by his power is present in the sacrament.[3]

The confessor's role is to mirror the love and compassion of God. The penitent may arrive broken-hearted, feeling cut off from God and full of confusion, shame and distress. In the confessor, the penitent should meet understanding, total acceptance and great encouragement. The confessor has to reflect to the penitent the very acceptance of God the Father and the forgiving love of Christ.

The specific grace of confession is this: people can bring to the sacrament all the sins, no matter how serious, for which they are sorry; they can confess them with the certainty that God forgives the sins and heals the wounds of sin; and they have the assurance that confidentiality is guaranteed. In the strictest sense, penitents can come to the sacrament and unburden themselves.

The healing power of the sacrament

When we go to the sacrament of reconciliation to confess our sins, it is the heart of God the Father that we encounter. God our Father has been patiently waiting for us, just as the father of the prodigal son in Jesus' parable was waiting for him to return home. In the parable the father was able to see his son while he was still far off. He was able to spot him at a distance because every day he was watching for his return. God the Father patiently waits for us to freely decide that we want to approach "the throne of grace and mercy", that we want to make our home in Christ. As the scripture says, "Let us therefore approach the throne of grace with boldness, so that we may receive mercy and find grace to help in time of need" (Hebrews 4:16). As we approach the throne of mercy, God our Father, like the father of the prodigal son, rushes to embrace us and fills us with the Holy Spirit.

---

3   *The Rite of Penance*, no. 10.

God, in his great love for us, gently reminds us that we are sinners and the deepest desire in his heart is that we welcome the grace of reconciliation, of forgiveness, that he offers us in the sacrament of confession. As St Paul said:

> If anyone is in Christ, there is a new creation: everything old has passed away; see, everything has become new! All this is from God, who reconciled us to himself through Christ, and has given us the ministry of reconciliation; that is, in Christ God was reconciling the world to himself, not counting their trespasses against them, and entrusting the message of reconciliation to us.
>
> 2 Corinthians 5:17-19

Every time we come to "the throne of grace and mercy" in the sacrament of confession, we are being freed from sin and "everything has become new". What an amazing revelation! God's mercy transforms our sinful hearts and makes them the very goodness of God. In the words of St Bernard, "God's mercy becomes my merit." Truly, that is the amazing mercy of God. From being sinners, turned in on ourselves, we become sharers in the very goodness of God, freed to go out in true love to others.

Purpose of amendment

True sorrow for sin includes the purpose of amendment, which puts our trust in God's mercy, despite all our weakness and sinfulness. The sacrament of confession is always a "sacrament of conversion", because it is only with a contrite spirit that we can approach "the throne of mercy". Pope St Paul VI describes conversion in this way:

> We can only approach the Kingdom of Christ by *metanoia*. This is a profound change of the whole person by which we begin to consider, judge, and arrange our life according to the holiness and love of God, made manifest in his Son in the last days and given to us in abundance. The genuineness of

penance depends on this heartfelt contrition. For conversion should affect a person from within toward a progressively deeper enlightenment and an ever-closer likeness to Christ.[4]

We receive that "deeper enlightenment" and we grow in "an ever-closer likeness to Christ" each time we celebrate the sacrament of reconciliation. This is a gift of grace, a gift of mercy. Cardinal Kasper writes, "Divine mercy grants sinners a period of grace and desires their conversion. Mercy is ultimately grace for conversion."[5] As St Bernard said:

> For my part, what I lack of myself I confidently take to myself from the compassionate heart of the Lord which flows with mercy and which is provided with outlets through which mercy flows. The mercy of the Lord is, then, my merit. I am never bereft of merit as long as he is not bereft of mercy.[6]

This gift enables us to say, "The mercy of God is my merit." God forgives all our sins in the sacrament of confession and, as the Psalm says, he "crowns [us] with steadfast love and mercy" (Psalm 103:4). We would be depriving ourselves of that wonderful richness of divine mercy if we didn't approach "the throne of grace and mercy". In the sacrament of confession we always experience the grace of conversion and we grow in "that ever-closer likeness to Christ". Jesus has left us free access to the "throne of grace and mercy". We can bring all our problems, our wounds and our sins to Christ in confession when we know we need some help and forgiveness.

Pope St Paul VI in his introduction to the *New Rite of Penance* focused on the healing power of the sacrament:

> In order that this sacrament of healing may truly achieve its purpose among Christ's faithful, it must take root in their whole lives and lead them to more fervent service of God and neighbour.[7]

---

4   St Paul VI, *The New Rite of Penance*, 6.
5   Cardinal Walter Kasper, *Mercy: the essence of the Gospel and the key to Christian life* (New York: Paulist Press, 2014), 54.
6   *Office of Readings*, Wednesday, Week 3.
7   *New Rite of Penance*, 7.

The sacrament of penance has a double function: the forgiveness of the sins that the penitent confesses and the healing of the wounds of sin that may have been inflicted on the penitent or which he or she has inflicted on themselves.

When we celebrate the sacrament of confession, we are saying to God and to ourselves that through the forgiveness of our sins we are determined to resist the temptation to sin again. To achieve this, we need a fresh infilling with the Holy Spirit. We know we can be very weak. St Peter is a good reminder for us. At the Last Supper Jesus said to Simon Peter, "Simon, Simon, listen! Satan has demanded to sift all of you like wheat, but I have prayed for you that your own faith may not fail; and you, when once you have turned back, strengthen your brothers." Peter said to him, "Lord, I am ready to go with you to prison and to death!" Jesus said, "I tell you, Peter, the cock will not crow this day, until you have denied three times that you know me" (Luke 22:31-34). And, as we know, in the courtyard of the high priest's palace the brave Peter did deny three times that he knew Jesus. When the cock crowed, Jesus, who was under arrest, turned and looked at Peter. Then Peter remembered what the Lord had said and "he went out and wept bitterly" (Luke 22:62). Peter remembered what the Lord had said: Satan was indeed sifting him. Jesus had warned him, but he felt so committed to Jesus that he couldn't even consider the possibility of Satan succeeding and causing him to deny that he knew the Lord.

Jesus knew that Peter would be very distressed by his denial that he ever knew him. After he rose from the dead, he revealed himself first of all to Peter. The disciples said to the couple who came back from Emmaus after seeing the risen Lord, "The Lord has risen indeed, and he has appeared to Simon!" (Luke 24:34).

When we confess our sins with "a firm purpose of amendment", that is, with the determination to avoid the sin in the future, with God's help, we are depending entirely on the grace of

God. Even if we fail again, as so often we do, we keep "the purpose of amendment" alive in our hearts. We begin again. The first principle of spiritual growth is to start again. The "purpose of amendment" keeps calling us back to the throne of mercy, where we hear again the words God spoke to St Paul: "My grace is sufficient for you, for power is made perfect in weakness" (2 Corinthians 12:9).

The wound of sin

What does the sacrament of confession heal? Pope St Paul VI answered that question in this way:

> Just as the wound of sin is varied and multiple in the life of individuals and of a community, so the healing which penance provides is varied.[8]

In celebrating the sacrament of confession with a contrite heart, our sins are forgiven and also the "wounds of our sins" are healed. But we have to pay attention to the fact that although God forgives us and takes away our sins, we may unconsciously refuse to forgive ourselves or forgive someone who has inflicted a hurt on us. When the Holy Spirit takes away our sins, he gives us the grace to humbly thank God for the gift of life. If we are not living in gratitude to God for our life, we will cultivate self-rejection and develop low self-esteem.

There is no inner emotional wound caused by sin that cannot be healed through the sacrament of reconciliation. We have in the sacrament God's healing for the whole Church. But the penitent must be led, by the light of the Spirit and by the gift of discernment, to recognise the nature of the wound. Without praying together and pondering the word of God together, as the rubrics of the sacrament require, the confessor and the penitent will have no light. There will be no discernment and very little healing.

---

8 *New Rite of Penance*, 7.

Wounds inflicted by the sins of others against us are also healed by the Holy Spirit in the sacrament of confession. We should always remember these words, which Jesus says to us about people who hurt us: "I say to you that listen, Love your enemies, do good to those who hate you, bless those who curse you, pray for those who abuse you" (Luke 6:27-28). Until we have the inner power to forgive those who have sinned against us, we will hold on to the wounds they have inflicted on our heart. These wounds rob us of love, joy and peace, the life-giving fruits of the Holy Spirit. If we go through life holding on to those inner wounds, we are inflicting an even deeper wound in our heart. We will find it difficult to make our home in Christ. We will be living in the home of the negative and destructive word.

So we see that the sacrament of confession not only obtains forgiveness for our own sins but also heals the wounds inflicted by our personal sins or those of others against us. We must bring these wounds to the Lord, lay them at his feet and thank him for giving us the grace to forgive. We must open our hearts to the Holy Spirit and leave all the inner hurts and wounds with the Spirit. Speaking about the Holy Spirit whom he was sending to us, Jesus says, "This is the Spirit of truth, whom the world cannot receive, because it neither sees him nor knows him. You know him, because he abides with you, and he will be in you" (John 14:17). We believe that the Holy Spirit is within us and wants to take away all our sins and heal the hurts that our sins have inflicted on us and on others. But we have to give the Holy Spirit the freedom to do all that. We have to ask the Spirit to create a loving and forgiving heart in us.

Sometimes I meet people who are conscientious about living a good life yet are holding on to a lack of forgiveness of the person or persons who have harmed them emotionally. A religious sister who as a young girl was sexually abused by her father for several years carried that wound in her heart for many years. Her mother knew all about what her father was doing, but didn't intervene to stop it. She escaped from her home by joining an order of religious sisters. She worked for years in mission in different parts of the world. She was due a time of rest and renewal and came for our seven-week sabbatical programme at St Mary's Monastery in Perth. One day, after I had celebrated midday Mass and preached on the fourth commandment, "Honour your father and your mother", she asked to see me. She told me the whole story of her childhood and how she could never honour her father because of his abuse or her mother for not protecting her. She looked me in the eye and said, "You wouldn't expect me to honour parents like that, would you?" I had full sympathy for her but I knew that the big hole in her heart was due to the absence of her forgiving love for her father and mother. I said to her, "I know God wants you to honour your parents and he wants to heal your heart so that you will be able to love them." Both parents were dead. She asked for prayer and I prayed over her, asking the Holy Spirit to bind up the wounds in her heart. Each evening we had the exposition of the Blessed Sacrament in the Oratory. She brought her inner wounds to the Lord as she adored the Blessed Sacrament. Then one evening she sensed her father coming into the Oratory, sitting beside her and joining in the adoration. A few evenings later she had a real sense of her mother too coming into the Oratory, sitting beside her and joining in the adoration. For a whole week she had the awareness of both parents sitting with her for her time of adoration. The wound in her heart was completely healed. She knew that she was filled with love for her parents; this was God's gift to her for her sabbatical time. She said to me, "Thank you for giving me back my parents." The liberating power of forgiveness from the heart heals even its deepest hurts.

How do we see sin?

In the *Catechism of the Catholic Church* we have this helpful definition of sin:

> Sin is an offence against reason, truth and right conscience; it is failure in genuine love of God and neighbour caused by a perverse attachment to certain goods. It wounds the nature of men and women and injures human solidarity. It has been defined as "an utterance, a deed or a desire contrary to the eternal life".[9]

In the first place, sin must be seen as an irrational act, "an offence against reason". It is contrary to our very nature, to our dignity as rational creatures whom God "has chosen for their own sake", to act in a totally selfish way. The Second Vatican Council said:

> The Lord Jesus, when praying to the Father "that they may all be one... even as we are one" (John 17:21-22), has opened up new horizons, closed to human reason, by indicating that there is a certain similarity between the union existing among the divine persons and the union of God's children in truth and love. It follows, then, that if human beings are the only creatures on earth that God has wanted for their own sake, they can fully discover their true selves only in sincere self-giving.[10]

Sin seeks to deny that we can discover our true selves by sincere self-giving. It tries to convince us that self-seeking, putting ourselves and our own interests before every other concern, is the only road to self-discovery and self-fulfilment. Our conscience, however, alerts us to the fact that all self-seeking ends ultimately in emptiness, in loneliness and in isolation. We can never discover our true self by self-seeking. Our true self is made in the image and likeness of God, who is self-giving. By refusing to be self-giving we would be refusing

---

9   *Catechism of the Catholic Church*, 1849.
10 Second Vatican Council, *Constitution on the Church in the Modern World*, 24.

to be like God. We would fail to actualise our deepest human power, which is the power to love. In the words of Pope St John Paul II, we have "the power to express love: precisely that love in which the human person becomes a gift – and through this gift – fulfils the very meaning of his or her being and existence".[11] That love is God's love; it is the love that "fulfils the very meaning of our being and existence"; the love with which we are empowered to love everyone in our life; the love that liberates us for self-giving. We protect this love and resist all temptation to withdraw it from any person because of his or her negative attitude towards us. We live by the words Jesus speaks: "But I say to you that listen, Love your enemies, do good to those who hate you, bless those who curse you, pray for those who abuse you" (Luke 6:27-28).

We have always regarded sin as an offence against God, but we haven't given much attention to the effect our own sins or those of others against us can have on ourselves, or the wounds that our sins against others can inflict on them. If we take the time to engage in a deeper examination of our conscience, asking ourselves, "Why did I react in that bad way?", we may begin to get in touch with a deep inner wound in our heart that has not yet healed. People can be totally unaware that the source of their negative attitudes is an inner wound that was inflicted on their heart years ago. That wound may be the cause of their self-seeking attitudes in relationships with others, which rob them of the joy of self-giving, the joy of discovering their true selves. God is self-giving and we, because we are made in the image and likeness of God, should reflect that self-giving by cultivating it in our own relationships. In the sacrament of penance we receive God's pardon for our sinful self-seeking but we may also often need the healing of an inner wound that is the cause of our self-seeking.

---

11 Pope St John Paul II, *Theology of the Body* (Boston, MA: Pauline Press, 2006), 15:1.

Discovering our true selves

The Second Vatican Council said:

> If human beings are the only creatures on earth that God has wanted for their own sake, they can fully discover their true selves only in sincere self-giving.[12]

Odd as it may sound, especially to our individualistic modern society, we would fail to discover our true self through self-seeking. Self-seeking would rob us of the joy of getting to know the self that God has made. God reveals himself to us in his sincere self-giving and, by our sincere self-giving in return, we discover our true selves as made in the image and likeness of the triune God. It is through sincere self-giving that we become like God. If we cultivate truthfulness, kindness, generosity, peacefulness and prayerfulness each day, we will become like God and we will learn that self-giving holds the secret of a happy and fulfilled life. When we fail to love from the heart, to love even our enemies, we hold on to inner wounds and we inflict yet more wounds on our heart. That is why Jesus says to us:

> Abide in me as I abide in you. Just as the branch cannot bear fruit by itself unless it abides in the vine, neither can you unless you abide in me. I am the vine, you are the branches. Those who abide in me and I in them bear much fruit, because apart from me you can do nothing.
>
> John 15:4-5

God our Father wants us to live happy and fulfilled lives. In giving us his Son, Jesus Christ, as our Saviour and Redeemer, our heavenly Father has opened for us the true meaning and purpose of our life in this world: it is our preparation for our eternal life with God in heaven. That is why Jesus invites us to abide in him, to make our home in him. The sacrament of confession that takes away all our sins purifies our inner

---

12 Second Vatican Council, *Constitution on the Church in the Modern World*, 24.

being and binds us in an ever-deeper union with God our Father, our Creator; with God the Son, our Lord Jesus Christ, our Redeemer; and with God the Holy Spirit, who sanctifies us and takes away all our sins. The sacrament of confession is the free gift from God for the cleansing and purification of our whole being, where God, Father, Son and Holy Spirit make their home. We can have no greater assurance of the abiding love of God than to be told that God the Father and the Son of God, Jesus our Redeemer, and the Holy Spirit, the Lord, the giver of life, make their home in us, in each one of us, as we do our best to make our home in Jesus.

Personal spiritual exercise for internalising the message of this chapter

- Centre yourself; sitting upright; breathing rhythmically; clearing your mind of all preoccupations.
- Bring yourself to bodily stillness.
- Now gratefully thank the Lord for his mercy and forgiveness.
- Experience the Father rushing to embrace you and welcome you.
- Be still for some time in the presence of the God of mercy and compassion and receive his love.
- Now focus again on your breathing as you relax in God's presence.
- And bring yourself gently back to the world.

This spiritual exercise will deepen your awareness of being in the presence of the God of grace and show you how God has embraced you with his love and mercy.

CHAPTER EIGHT

JESUS' LAST WORDS TO US FROM THE CROSS: "SHE IS YOUR MOTHER"

In the Gospel of John we find this scene on Calvary: "When Jesus saw his mother and the disciple whom he loved standing beside her, he said to his mother, 'Woman, here is your son'. Then he said to the disciple, 'Here is your mother'. And from that hour the disciple took her into his own home" (John 19:26-27). That disciple represents every disciple of Jesus. As St Alphonsus Liguori said:

> Here observe well that Jesus Christ did not address himself to John, but to the disciple, in order to show that he gave Mary to all who are his disciples, that is to say to all Christians, that she might be their mother. John is but the name of one, whereas the word disciple is applicable to all; therefore our Lord makes use of a name common to all, to show that Mary was given as mother to all.[1]

You too are a disciple, so to you Jesus says, "She is your mother." We thank Jesus for this astounding gift of his own holy mother to be our holy mother, to be the holy mother of all those who believe in Jesus and, indeed, for all those who as yet have never heard of Jesus. As the disciples of Jesus we have a mission to be witnesses to him; his mother Mary will help us to do that.

St John's statement, "When Jesus saw his mother...", is very significant. What did Jesus see as he gazed from the cross at his mother? He saw not just his own beloved biological mother but also the spiritual mother of his disciple as he stood at the foot of his cross. He saw the mother of all his disciples, of his Church, which was coming to birth through his death and resurrection. Jesus sees in his mother a new maternity, a spiritual one. He reveals to his mother what he sees with the words: "Woman, here is your son."

---

1 Alphonsus Liguori, *Classics of Western Spirituality* (New York: Paulist Press, 1999), 26.

Mary didn't know that she was to become the spiritual mother of the disciple until God revealed it to her through the words of her dying son. Jesus' last words to his mother are about her new motherhood of his disciples. This is a new revelation that Jesus is giving to her. When the angel Gabriel said to Mary, "The Holy Spirit will come upon you, and the power of the Most High will overshadow you; therefore the child to be born will be holy; he will be called Son of God," Mary said, "Here am I, the servant of the Lord; let it be with me according to your word" (Luke 1:35-38). Mary now makes the same response to this new revelation that Jesus gives her from the cross just before he dies: "Here am I, the servant of the Lord; let it be with me according to your word." Now Mary will live by this word of God spoken to her by her son Jesus. By the power of that word of God Mary becomes the mother of the disciple, and thus the mother of all disciples. And we know that Mary, the mother of Jesus and our spiritual mother, is our best teacher on how to make our home in her beloved son.

Devotion to Mary

Being devoted to Mary doesn't mean being devoted to her memory, to the fact that she was the mother of Jesus, but being devoted to her person, to the one who is the mother of Jesus today and who has been appointed *our* mother by Jesus from the cross. She is present today in the mystery of Christ and the Church. As Pope St John Paul II wrote:

> Mary is present in the Church as the Mother of Christ, and at the same time as that mother whom Christ, in the mystery of the Redemption, gave to humanity in the person of the Apostle John. Thus, in her new motherhood in the Spirit, Mary embraces each and every one *in* the Church, and embraces each and every one *through* the Church.[2]

---

[2] Pope St John Paul II, *Redemptoris Mater* ("Mother of the Redeemer"), 47.

Devotion to Mary involves a relationship with a living, loving person, present in our lives, whom we acknowledge to be our mother in the Spirit. Mary, now totally alive in God, is present to us in God, as Mother of Christ and mother of the Church, the Mystical Body of Christ. Her maternal presence fills us with confidence and hope. We know we can trust her. Pope St John Paul II said:

> For it must be recognized that before anyone else it was God himself, the Eternal Father, who *entrusted himself to the Virgin of Nazareth,* giving her his own Son in the mystery of the Incarnation.[3]

This remarkable teaching focuses on the reality behind all devotion to Mary: God the Father trusted her and entrusted his Son to her. Our devotion is a sign that we too trust her and that we entrust ourselves to her.

Reflecting on Mary's presence on Calvary, the Second Vatican Council said:

> Thus the Blessed Virgin advanced in her pilgrimage of faith, and faithfully persevered in her union with her Son until she stood at the foot of the cross, in keeping with the divine plan (see John 19:25), suffering deeply with her only begotten Son, associating herself with his sacrifice in her mother's heart, and lovingly consenting to the immolation of this victim who was born of her. Finally, she was given by the same Christ Jesus dying on the cross as a mother to his disciple, with these words: "Woman, this is your Son."(John 19:26-27)[4]

Jesus then looks from the cross at his beloved disciple, and what does he see? He sees, of course, this disciple whom he loves, his true follower. But he sees something else. He sees that this disciple, and all future disciples, will have his mother Mary as their holy mother. They become his brothers and sisters. As the Vatican Council said:

---

3 Pope St John Paul II, *Redemptoris Mater*, 39.
4 Second Vatican Council, *Dogmatic Constitution on the Church*, 58.

For, by his incarnation, he, the Son of God, has in a certain way united himself with each individual.[5]

Through the redemptive words of Jesus, spoken from the cross, the disciple comes into a new relationship with Jesus, his Master. The sign of that new relationship is that both are sons of the same mother: Jesus in his humanity is the son of Mary; the disciple in his redeemed humanity is also the spiritual son of Mary. How does the disciple respond? John records, "From that hour the disciple took her into his own home" (John 19:27).

John McHugh, a great expert on John's Gospel, wrote:

> John 19:27 seems to demand a translation, which includes both the purely physical and the deeper, spiritual sense. "And from that hour the disciple took her into his own home and accepted her as his own mother, as part of the spiritual legacy bequeathed to him by the Lord."[6]

Pope Benedict XVI agrees with McHugh:

> The literal translation is stronger still; it could be rendered like this: he took her into his own – received her into his inner life-setting.[7]

The disciple made physical space for Mary in his home, but more profoundly he accepted her into his own life as his mother.

Mary's presence on Calvary, and the words Jesus spoke to her, are recorded only in John's Gospel. Matthew and more especially Luke tell us about the birth and the infancy of Jesus, but they don't mention Mary's presence on Calvary. John tells us why he mentioned it:

> Now Jesus did many other signs in the presence of his disciples, which are not written in this book. But these are written so that you may come to believe that Jesus is the Messiah, the Son of God, and that through believing you may have life in his name.
>
> John 20:30-31

---

5 Second Vatican Council, *Constitution on the Church in the Modern World*, 22.
6 John McHugh, *The Mother of Jesus in the New Testament* (London: Darton, Longman & Todd, 1975), 378.
7 Pope Benedict XVI, *Jesus of Nazareth, Part 2* (London: Catholic Truth Society, 2011), 221.

Mother of Mercy

One of those signs that Jesus gave was to declare that his holy mother has become our holy mother too. John is making it very clear, then, that Mary's presence on Calvary and Jesus' words to her are recorded so that we might believe. We cannot pass over this presence of Mary at the foot of the cross on Calvary, when Jesus proclaimed to the beloved disciple, "She is your mother", as if those words are not addressed to us. Those living words of God are meant for us today, just as much as they were spoken to the disciple at the foot of the cross. We don't just hear the words but, as Jesus says, we "[live] by every word that comes from the mouth of God" (Matthew 4:4). That comforting and life-transforming statement, "She is your mother", comes from the mouth of God and we embrace it; we live by it.

In the Church, down through the centuries, we have devised many forms of devotion for honouring Our Blessed Lady. One of the best-loved and most cherished antiphons to Mary is the *Salve Regina,* the Hail, Holy Queen, in which the Church gives Our Lady the title "Mother of Mercy". This antiphon is sung or said at Compline, the night prayer of the Church, from the Saturday before Trinity Sunday until the Friday before the first Sunday of Advent. For more than half the year, then, in her official night prayer, the Church acclaims Mary as Mother of Mercy. It dates from around the twelfth century. Those who don't use the liturgical prayer of Compline would know this prayer as the concluding part of the rosary. We remind ourselves of the words of this ancient antiphon:

> Hail, Holy Queen, Mother of Mercy,
> hail our life, our sweetness and our hope.
> To thee do we cry poor banished children of Eve,
> to thee do we send up our sighs,
> mourning and weeping in this vale of tears.
> Turn, then, most gracious Advocate, thine eyes of mercy towards us and after this our exile show unto us the blessed fruit of thy womb, Jesus.
> O clement, O loving, O sweet Virgin Mary.

Versicle - Pray for us, O Holy Mother of God
Response - That we may be made worthy of the promises of Christ.

St Alphonsus and The Glories of Mary

St Alphonsus Liguori, one of the great Marian saints of the Church, based his most popular book, *The Glories of Mary,* on the Hail, Holy Queen. This book has been translated into over eighty different languages and appeared in over 800 known editions. In his introduction he tells us modestly:

> I leave to other authors to praise the other prerogatives of Mary and I confine myself, for the most part, to her mercy and the power of her intercession. I have gathered, as far as I was able (and it was the work of many years), all that the Fathers of the Church and the most celebrated authors have to say on the subject. I find that the mercy and power of Our Lady are admirably portrayed in the prayer *Salve Regina* (Hail, Holy Queen).[8]

No book on Mary has been as widely distributed or as deeply appreciated as *The Glories of Mary*. Saints and scholars, learned and unlearned alike, have all found comfort and encouragement in this Marian classic. Alphonsus wanted the faithful to read the very best literature on Mary. That is why he worked for over twenty years on gathering the material for his book. It is a work of immense scholarship and devotion. As Frederick Jones, in his biography of St Alphonsus, wrote:

> Beneath the apparently devotional form of *The Glories of Mary* lies a rich mine of sound theological teaching on the Mother of God. As a positive contribution to the Mariological section of theology, it marked a decisive stage in the doctrinal evolution of the doctrine of Our Lady's Immaculate Conception.[9]

---

8   St Alphonsus Liguori, *The Glories of Mary* (Liguori, MO: Salve Regina, 2002), xxiii.
9   Frederick Jones, *Alphonsus de Liguori: The Saint of Bourbon Naples 1696-1787* (Dublin: Gill & Macmillan, 1992), 274.

Pope St John Paul II, speaking about the legacy of St Alphonsus, said:

> St. Alphonsus is a gigantic figure, not only in the history of the Church, but for the whole of humanity as well. Even people who would not follow his vision, still see in him "the teacher of the Catholic soul of the West". He did for modern Catholicism that which Augustine accomplished in ancient times.[10]

Speaking of *The Glories of Mary*, Pope Francis said, "In this book, I like reading the stories about Mary that are at the end of each chapter; in them we see how Mary always leads us to Jesus."[11] Jesus, from the cross, commissioned his mother to do precisely that: to be the mother of all his disciples and to bring them all to him. That is why we can say that devotion to Mary, whatever form it takes, protects our faith in the divinity of her son and helps us to make our home in Jesus.

Jesus came to redeem the human race, and his mother now joins him in that mission. Mary became the Mother of Mercy. As such, Mary seeks to support each human being. She loves us and guides and supports each daughter or son who asks for her help. Mary never refuses a cry for help. As our loving mother, she presents us to her son Jesus and to God the Father and asks for a fresh outpouring of the Holy Spirit on the daughter or son who has turned to her for help.

In the hour of God's merciful redemption, Mary became the mother of all the disciples of Jesus. She was the herald of God's mercy to her cousin Elizabeth. When Elizabeth, filled with the Holy Spirit, cried out, "Of all women you are the most blessed, and blessed is the fruit of your womb. Why should I be honoured with a visit from the mother of my Lord? For the moment your greeting reached my ears, the child in my womb leapt for joy. Yes, blessed is she who believed that the promise made her by the Lord would be fulfilled" (Luke 1:42-45, NJB), Mary responded to Elizabeth with her wonderful Magnificat, in which she explains what is going on in her life:

---

10 St Alphonsus Liguori, *Classics of Western Spirituality* (New York: Paulist Press, 1999), 51.
11 Pope St John Paul II, Catholic News Service, 16 April 2015.

> My soul magnifies the Lord,
> and my spirit rejoices in God my Saviour,
> for he has looked with favour on the lowliness of his servant.
> Surely, from now on all generations will call me blessed;
> for the Mighty One has done great things for me,
> and holy is his name.
> His mercy is for those who fear him from generation to generation.
> He has shown strength with his arm;
> he has scattered the proud in the thoughts of their hearts.
> He has brought down the powerful from their thrones,
> and lifted up the lowly;
> he has filled the hungry with good things,
> and sent the rich away empty.
> He has helped his servant Israel, in remembrance of his mercy,
> according to the promise he made to our ancestors,
> to Abraham, and to his descendants for ever.
>
> Luke 1:46-55

Mary understands that the incarnation of her son Jesus Christ in her womb is the act in which God remembers his mercy. Pope Francis expresses this well when he writes:

> Jesus Christ is the face of the Father's mercy. These words might well sum up the mystery of Christian faith. Mercy has become living and visible in Jesus of Nazareth, reaching its culmination in him.[12]

As the mother of Jesus, Mary gave birth to the "mercy of God incarnate". She suckled and nursed the mercy of God; she taught "the mercy of God incarnate" how to say his prayers as a child. And, as Jesus "increased in wisdom, in stature, and in favour with God and men" (Luke 2:52, NJB), Mary continued to mother him. God had given her all the divine help she needed to be the mother of his Divine Mercy.

---

12 Pope Francis, *Bull of Indiction of Extraordinary Jubilee of Mercy*, 1.

Our Lady's presence in the Church

Devotion to Our Blessed Lady is based on the word of God. It is our response to Jesus' last words to his beloved disciple and the fulfilment of Mary's own prophecy: "From now on all generations will call me blessed" (Luke 1:48). Jesus' last word to his disciple, his last will and testament, was expressed in the words "She is your mother". In a very striking comment on these words, Pope St John Paul II said, "It can be said that by asking the beloved disciple to treat Mary as his mother, Jesus founded Marian devotion."[13] Jesus asked his beloved disciple to be devoted to his mother, to have the same love, care and respect for Mary that he himself had. That is the original meaning of the word "devotion". We often speak of someone being very devoted to their father or mother. Devotion involves thinking about, being attentive to, caring for, spending time with.

The disciple makes a place for Mary in his home (John 19:27). She is present as mother in the life of each disciple of Jesus. You are a disciple and therefore Mary, the Mother of God and your spiritual mother, is present in your life. The disciple's response to her presence in his spiritual life is one of devotion; love and gratitude for her constant care; trust in her powerful intercession in times of need; great confidence in her as our Mother of Perpetual Help.

Our Lady is never absent from the Church nor from the experience of the faithful. Mary, our Mother of Mercy, embraces us with the divine love and mercy with which the Holy Spirit has filled her whole being in abundance.

Mary our spiritual mother has a personal relationship with each of us. Catholics believe that she was assumed body and soul into heaven and crowned the Queen of Heaven and Earth. She relates personally with each of us.

---

13 *L'Osservatore Romano, English Weekly Edition*, 11 May 1983.

The act of entrustment

Jesus entrusts each of us to the love and care of his mother. Many Catholics who give up the practice of their religion hold on to a love for the mother of Jesus. Deep down in their heart they yearn for their mother. When their life becomes difficult, through sickness or the loss of their job or serious trouble in a relationship, many of them turn to their heavenly mother with a thought or a glance or a silent prayer in their heart. They begin to remember that Mary is their mother, a gift that Jesus gives to each person. Then they begin to discover that Mary is at their side throughout all their troubles. She doesn't condemn or find fault. She is there to encourage, to help, to renew. And if the person in need of her motherly help can entrust himself or herself to her, she will be able to fill them with hope, heal their inner wounds and lead them on the path of inner peace. They are never disappointed. We honour Jesus when we entrust ourselves to his holy mother. We can turn to her in our every need and receive her maternal care.

One of the distinguishing features of Catholic spirituality is devotion to Our Blessed Lady. It began when the disciple at the foot of the cross, as Pope Benedict XVI said, "took her into his own – received her into his inner life-setting".[14] The Church recognises that Mary so associated herself with Jesus on the cross that she suffered in her heart what he was suffering in his body. Mary became the mother of "the beloved disciple" in the awesome hour of the crucifixion of Jesus. As Pope St John Paul II says:

> This "new motherhood of Mary", generated by faith, is *the fruit of the "new" love* which came to definitive maturity in her at the foot of the Cross, through her sharing in the redemptive love of her son.[15]

---

14 Pope Benedict XVI, *Jesus of Nazareth, Part 2* (London: Catholic Truth Society, 2011), 221.
15 St John Paul II, *Redemptoris Mater*, 25 March 1987.

Christ's faithful have always recognised that we have a special relationship with the mother of Jesus: the relationship of daughters and sons to their mother in faith. We have engaged in a great variety of different devotional practices to foster our relationship with our Mother of Mercy. There are many beautiful prayers to Our Lady that have been handed on from one generation to the next. This is one of my favourite prayers that I say each day to our heavenly mother Mary:

> Most Holy Virgin Mary, perfect disciple of Jesus, I come to dedicate my life and my priestly ministry to your Immaculate Heart. I desire to abandon myself to the will of Jesus, your Son, and walk in faith with you, my mother. To you I consecrate my life in the priesthood. I give you every gift I possess of nature and of grace – my body and soul; all that I have and everything I do. Pray for me, that the Holy Spirit may visit me with God's many gifts. Pray with me, that by faith I may know the power of Christ and by love make him present in the world.

You can adapt that prayer to your own vocation in life and say, "I dedicate my marriage and my family life to your Immaculate Heart," or "I dedicate my life in my retirement to your Immaculate Heart," or "I dedicate this day to your Immaculate Heart." This prayer of entrustment of oneself to our Mother of Mercy is our grateful acceptance of the gift that Jesus gives to each of us when he says to us, "She is your mother." These words from the cross, spoken to his beloved disciple, explain the Marian dimension of the life of Christ's disciples. Pope St John Paul II, in his encyclical on "The Mother of the Redeemer", wrote:

> The Redeemer entrusts his mother to the disciple, and at the same time he gives her to him as his mother. Mary's motherhood, which becomes man's inheritance, is a gift: a gift which Christ himself makes personally to every individual. The Redeemer entrusts Mary to John because he entrusts John to Mary. At the foot of the Cross there begins

that special entrusting of humanity to the Mother of Christ, which in the history of the Church has been practiced and expressed in different ways.[16]

Since Jesus entrusted each of us to the love and care of his mother, we can practise no better devotion than to freely and gratefully entrust ourselves to Mary, our spiritual mother. In a very formal way Pope St John Paul II, in union with all the bishops of the Catholic Church, entrusted the whole world to the Immaculate Heart of Mary on 25 March 1984. That was a solemn act of the whole church. This is just one of the prayers of dedication that St John Paul gave:

> Behold, as we stand before you, Mother of Christ, before your immaculate Heart, we desire, together with the whole Church, to unite ourselves with the consecration which for love of us, your Son made of himself to the Father. "For their sake", he said, I consecrate myself that they also may be consecrated in the truth" (John 17:19). When we entrust ourselves to Mother Mary, in a personal act of commitment and dedication, we are accepting that, in God's plan for his people, Mary, the mother of Jesus and our mother, is the mother who cares for each human being. We are invited to join our Mother of Perpetual Help as we pray for our human race. And, as we honour Mary, the mother of Jesus and our mother, she responds by helping us to make our home in Jesus her son.

While we are on this earth, Mary our mother directs all our spiritual struggles to her son Jesus and asks him to make a home for us in his life. Jesus fulfils that great request when he says, "Those who love me will keep my word, and my Father will love them, and we will come to them and make our home with them" (John 14:23). Our mother Mary will always be at our side, encouraging us to make our home in Jesus and to welcome the Father and Jesus into our hearts.

---

16 Pope St John Paul II, *Redemptoris Mater*, 45.

Personal spiritual exercise for internalising the message of this chapter

- Centre yourself; sitting upright; breathing rhythmically; clearing your mind of all preoccupations.
- Bring yourself to bodily stillness.
- Calmly listen to the words of Jesus from the cross: "She is your mother." Now humbly and gratefully accept Mary, the mother of Jesus, as your spiritual mother and ask for her prayers and help.
- Be still for some time in the presence of Jesus and Mary.
- Now focus again on your breathing as you relax in God's presence.
- And bring yourself gently back to the world.

This spiritual exercise will deepen your awareness of being in the presence of the God of grace and show you how God has embraced you with his love and mercy.